The State of Freedom and Justice

'He will not falter or be discouraged till
he establishes justice on earth.'

Isaiah 42:4

The State
of
Freedom
and
Justice

Government
as if
PEOPLE MATTER MOST

MICHAEL HORSMAN

SHEPHEARD-WALWYN (PUBLISHERS) LTD

First published in 2016 by
Shepheard-Walwyn (Publishers) Ltd
107 Parkway House, Sheen Lane,
London SW14 8LS
www.shepheard-walwyn.co.uk

British Library Cataloguing in Publication Data
A catalogue record of this book
is available from the British Library

ISBN: 978-0-85683-510-0

Typeset by Alacrity, Chesterfield, Sandford, Somerset
Printed and bound in the United Kingdom
by Short Run Press, Exeter

Contents

Foreword

IS POLITICS really all about left versus right? Over the last hundred or more years it has become the practice to grade political proposals and people as ranging across a spectrum from communism, socialism and left wing, through centre, to right wing, fascism and anarchism. How useful, real or objective is this spectrum, or is it simply a tool with which to divide and conquer? Do we actually gain useful information from these descriptions, or is the real winner the *'father of lies'*, while good-hearted men are set against good-hearted men, and so the war goes on?

To illustrate the problem of using this method of political analysis, consider the following. Generally speaking, increased taxes of all types are considered left wing, while lower taxes and lower tax rates are right wing. So any proposition that sets out to abolish all taxes – except one – is likely to be considered far right. On the other hand, individual property rights are usually considered right wing while common rights to property are thought of as left wing. So any proposal that would make natural resources ('Land', to use the economist's term) common property, is likely to be considered far left if not outright communism.

What then if the first proposal above (the far right one) to remove all taxes is combined with the 'Single Tax' on Land values – which would essentially make Land common property – is such a proposal left wing or right wing or centre? Does the addition of a far right proposal with a far left make a centrist proposal? Or have we transcended the definition of left and right, showing that paradigm to be worse than useless: actually petty and divisive?

Consider another example: Big government involvement in health, education and welfare are normally considered left wing, while small government is considered right wing. Therefore, any proposal to pare

1

government down to defence, police and justice only – getting rid of any and all State involvement in health, education and welfare – is likely to be considered extreme right wing. On the other hand, a proposal to turn the judicial system into a judicial *service* which provides free legal services to all may be considered left wing or extreme left.

Again we can ask the question: what if these two extreme propositions are combined? Have we arrived at some populist, centrist position or have we simply shown the left/right spectrum to be a false, divisive and useless way of looking at the political scene?

To underline this question, what if we combine all four of the above proposals together? Extreme right: Abolish all taxes on production and limit government to police, defence and justice. Extreme left: Tax Land values only and institute a free judicial service. Clearly these proposals shatter the right/left spectrum and demonstrate the need for a new way of looking at politics. So if politics is not left or right, then what is it? What is an objective and useful measure of politics, politicians and their proposals?

Ronald Reagan, when on the stump for Barry Goldwater in 1964, gave a speech then titled 'A Time for Choosing' but which has become known simply as 'The Speech', in which he said, *'You and I are told increasingly we have to choose between a left or right. Well I'd like to suggest there is no such thing as a left or right. There's only an up or down: up, man's old, age-old dream, the ultimate in individual freedom consistent with law and order, or down to the ant heap of totalitarianism'.* In these few words we have the real perspective for political analysis. Both right wing and left wing end up in totalitarianism, the 'down' of the anthill. The opposite pole is freedom – the 'up' at which we must aim.

Now freedom is normally couched in the context of 'freedom from something', as in freedom from slavery; something negative. Rarely do we consider freedom in the positive sense 'freedom *for* something', so we would do well to put it as a question: freedom for what? In this sense, we normally hear the word 'individualism' used, and an answer such as: *'Freedom for the individual to pursue his own ends without treading on the equal freedoms of others.'* This individualistic perspective on freedom is accurate but misleading in a very important sense. Individualism never has been – nor can ever be – the atomistic isolationism that this word would conjure up, like the lone gold digger working the wild mountains and streams. True and successful individualism is always socially cooperative and responsible; it is family, friends and partners, it is church, tribe, clan, club, it is shipmates, colony of pioneers, the firm, it is the company, voluntary self-help organisation and voluntary 'other-help' organisations. Individualism is *always* social and cooperative, *mostly* it is responsible. To take care of those in need around you is actually long-sighted caring for yourself: one day you may be in need and the measure with which you have given is the measure with which you will be given. Even the baboons have worked that one out! The making of friends is very important in baboon society for exactly this reason.

The ultimate in human freedom is thus the high calling of responsible, cooperative individualism. This kind of freedom is the one pole of politics, the 'up' in Reagan's speech. The polar opposite is the 'down' that we have the world over today – State-ism of varying degrees – all the way down to the totalitarianism of China, Saudi Arabia, North Korea or Iran. The 'up' of freedom or the 'down' of totalitarianism, this is the true perspective of politics, not left or right as we have it now.

Reagan went on to say '*And regardless of their sincerity – their humani-tarian motives – those who would trade our freedom for security have embarked on this downward course.*' No matter how good their *apparent* motives, those (whether from the right or left) who would urge the government or State to use its power to do anything beyond defence, police and justice, are those who would play God, who wish to control the lives of others, to mould and shape others according to their own prideful thoughts.

God has created nature; human and non-human nature. Those in positions of power have only to observe the Laws of nature, written into the universe and written in the nature of man, to see that the role of the State is really very small and that man knows best how to live, adapt and thrive when left to choose for himself. When he is free.

For thousands of years, Man and the State have wrestled with one another to find which will be the winner: freedom or totalitarianism. This book is the result of a three decade long effort to understand and demonstrate the principles which lead to the smallest and most tightly constrained State. Is this the theoretical foundation for maximum freedom; the highest possible 'up'? Is the fight nearly over?

Introduction

*'It often happens that a quick opinion inclines in the
wrong direction and after that the intellect
is hampered by vanity.'*

Dante, *The Divine Comedy*

THIS BOOK was born of a youthful attempt to sort out ideas about
politics and government from the confused and confusing array of
policies practiced or offered around the world. There was no intention of
writing a book; it was simply an effort to lay out the principles underlying
the State and government; principles so clearly and beautifully displayed
by the rest of creation but which seemed thus far to have evaded all efforts
to expose or capture in this field.

The first problem to present itself was the issue of taxation, a problem
which seems to confound every Minister of Finance to this day. In the
aftermath of the crash of 2007/8, State treasuries floundered about not
knowing what to do to cope with the economic crisis. Some countries
have done one thing such as increase taxes, others the exact opposite without any discernible effect. Some have done one thing and then reversed
course as Ireland did in 2010: in the spring the Minister of Finance reduced
VAT from 21% to 20%, the following winter the very same man put it back
up to 21%! This only goes to show that those whom we trust in these
powerful positions do not have a clue. It is as if they toss a coin to make
their decisions.

The perspective from which I chose to study taxation was to look
simply and solely at the negative or disincentive effects of every form of
tax I could research. At the end of the search I could find only one 'tax'
that had a positive or beneficial economic effect. This conclusion was
confirmed shortly after by the discovery that someone had already written

an economic bestseller on exactly this idea, but today he has been buried by those who don't want the truth to be told. On finding that an international organisation devoted to disseminating this truth had existed for over a hundred years, but that it was marginal in its influence, I wrote and published what has become Chapter 4 of this book. Sensing this barrier to success I then faced the more difficult question: if the problem of raising revenue had been solved intellectually, what did this mean for the other side of government, its expenditure? What should the functions of the State be? The answer to this would take most of twenty-five years to work out, and this book is the result. So what is in it?

Part I is background discussion (setting the scene) beginning with defining some terms such as, capitalism, freedom, justice and the market in Chapter 1. Then we take an in-depth look at the history of the State and the conflicting theories of its origins in Chapter 2. Finally, in Chapter 3, we enter the realm of natural Law to see what it says concerning the State and government. Here we find a solid foundation from which we can go on to construct all the principles necessary for the State of Freedom and Justice.

Part II is the main body of this work, a chapter each on the three main proposals: the Single Tax, Chapter 4, the Minimal State, Chapter 5, and the Judicial Service, Chapter 6.

Part III is an acknowledgement that the three main proposals – the Minimal State particularly – are truly sweeping and would make dramatic changes to society and the social order. Life without the State, Chapter 7, and Money, Banking and the Trade Cycle, Chapter 8, address the question of how most current State services would be performed by private enterprise; performed so much better too.

Finally Part IV tackles both the moral issues connected with these proposals and the practical issues concerning their implementation. Heaven on Earth, Chapter 9, discusses the link between political action and Divine will. The last chapter, Wither the State!, Chapter 10, paints a picture of how to achieve the three main objectives of this book over the lifetime of a government, describing the most efficient and least disruptive method and order for implementing these reforms.

*

Most people date the collapse of communism in Europe to the collapse of the Berlin wall on the 9th November 1989. I prefer to date it with the following statement by long term communist apologist, Robert

Heilbroner, in an article in *The New Yorker* dated January 1989, just a few months earlier.

> Less than 75 years after it officially began, the contest between capitalism and socialism is over; capitalism has won. The Soviet Union, China, and eastern Europe have given us the clearest possible proof that capitalism organises the material affairs of humankind more satisfactorily than socialism ... Indeed, it is difficult to observe the changes taking place in the world today and not conclude that the nose of the capitalist camel has been pushed so far under the socialist tent that the great question now seems to be, how rapidly will the transformation from socialism to capitalism occur, – and not the other way around as things looked only a half century ago.

The Iron Curtain melted in the minds of its creators and protagonists before it collapsed in reality, and the result was that many people caught a breath of freedom that they had been denied for generations. Capitalism had become no longer, a dirty word, and many other nations around the world embraced it along with its necessary condition – freedom.

The two decades that followed saw the appearance of a global economy unlike any that has ever existed before. Capitalism and freedom united the labours of literally billions of people all across the globe allowing the benefits of specialisation to touch those who partook. The communist experiment failed and capitalism danced on its grave for nearly a generation. But this capitalism and freedom has a fatal flaw, one that prevents the continuous flow of its bounty to all its participants. Rather it booms and slumps with the reliability of 'Old Faithful' –Yellowstone Park's famous geyser – regularly shattering the hopes, dreams and lives of almost everyone. Some never recover from these shocks.

So what is the fatal flaw and how can it be fixed? How can the amazing energy of free people, cooperating voluntarily to produce staggering quantities of wealth be so focused as to deliver on a sustained and sustainable basis – and delivered in a fair and just manner? Clearly the boom time has within itself the seeds of its own crash. We must figure out how capitalism works, what these seeds are and why and how it fails so many, so consistently. Can we find and correct the flaws of this capitalism and promise a bright future for all people, always and everywhere? This book is a clear yes to that question, providing a new vision of capitalism – one that harnesses the creative energies of each individual to its optimum, while avoiding the fundamental problem of modern economies.

In the final analysis, this book is about belief: belief that a solution to our problems exist – it is practical and it is possible. Either we believe that the universe is built on reason and order, and that we are destined to master its systems, or we believe that it is built on chaos and random, and will forever be the domain of the insane. The choice is as stark and dramatic as that – you must decide which you believe.

The focus of this book is government and the structure and function of the State, but I do not think you will find it as dreary a subject as it is traditionally assumed to be. You are unlikely to be familiar with any of the proposals put forward and they may just take your breath away with their promise of sweeping change. They may even make you feel like walking on air, so unfamiliar are they to our normal concept of government and the State. Yet there are few ideas in this book that are new; all the main proposals have been documented and championed in the past. Like treasures of knowledge, these have been kept hidden; I have had the amazing experience of discovering them one by one, while my contribution has been to bring them all together as a neatly fitting whole. No one that I know of has championed all these ideas as one package, and sometimes I have felt like the rabbit in *Alice in Wonderland* who could easily believe half a dozen impossible things before breakfast!

Although the main proposals in the book are not new, I can claim to have worked out two of them – the Single Tax and the free Judicial service – for myself. Those were great moments of confirmation for my thought journey when I found that Henry George and Herbert Spencer respectively had gotten there long before me. It was confirmation I greatly valued as I found myself on this otherwise lonely voyage.

As far as I know, I am unique in deriving both the two main proposals from one principle. The natural, unalienable, God-given right of individuals to property and to self-defence respectively lead to the Single Tax and the Minimal State. This means they are two parts of the one whole. They are actually one *indivisible* idea so one cannot exist without the other. Also I can find no other who would claim that a sound money and banking system requires the Single Tax. This last and most recent insight has enormous implications, for it suggests a whole new, powerful and moneyed interest in getting the proposals of this book enacted. Thus the 'too-big-to-fail' financial system has a self-interest in seeing these proposals implemented. Two other original contributions are (i) the self-regulating mechanism of the revenue source (Horsman's homeostatic principle) and (ii) the middle way between the US and British 'division of powers' between the legislature and the executive.

It is all very well to put forward a bold new plan, but if it is to happen we must believe that change can occur. History shows that change in States can happen both violently and peacefully. The so-called 'Arab Spring' has bloodily changed many Arab nations. Recent European history witnessed the dramatic but peaceful changes when communism collapsed, and we can be assured that even more dramatic changes can still occur. Man is the author of States, and this generation has as much right to script its own States as past generations have done to create the present ones.

PART I

Deep Background

CHAPTER 1

Capitalism, Freedom, Justice and the Market

'...words, like nature,
half reveal and half conceal
the soul within.'

Alfred Tennyson, In Memoriam

Capitalism

P ROFESSOR HEILBRONER'S use of the word 'capitalism', looking forward to its victory over communism (see Introduction), reveals a problem of definition that is not just semantic. In the sense that he uses it, Heilbroner means 'that which is opposed to communism'; in this way capitalism has been demonised by its opponents to conjure up all that is bad in the world. Unfortunately it has become the accepted term even by its proponents, demonstrating the fact that a good philosophical underpinning for this vision does not yet exist.

Capitalism in its purest meaning is the use of tools (machines, systems, energy, as well as money) to produce goods. One who digs a hole with his hands is not yet a capitalist; one who digs with a spade is the primordial capitalist; one who digs with a mechanised digger is the archetypal capitalist; while someone who heads a corporation that removes thousands of tonnes of raw material from the earth is the capitalist that socialists love to hate.

The spade is a tool that can be fashioned using simple technology and is therefore not dependent on a sophisticated political and economic system. The mechanical digger can be manufactured only under a complex economic system, and this in turn can exist only under a certain style of political system. This holds true and is even more critical for the large corporation. For this reason capitalism has come to denote a certain type of political system, and perhaps this is why it is used more frequently in a political sense. But the use of the economic term 'capitalism' for a political system is really an overstretch.

In this original, economic sense of the word, communism is also capitalism. The only difference is that under communism all the means of production are owned by the State and so it is really State capitalism. When, therefore, socialists use the term capitalism, what they really mean is *the political system which protects the private ownership of Capital*, a system abhorred by the socialists. What they are really objecting to is the private ownership of the tools of production.

The use of the *economic term* 'capitalism' to denote the *political system* that protects private ownership of Capital, reveals an enormous void in the philosophy that underpins this political system. It is not the *use* of tools that is being described, it is *how the tools are owned* or legally held that is at issue. That this misnomer – coined by the opposition – is used freely by those who wish to secure private ownership of Capital, reveals the absence of a clear philosophical underpin. This lack of underpinning leaves it open to future attacks by communist or other Statist fallacies.

The argument, sometimes used by defenders of capitalism, that capitalism does not need a coherent philosophy because 'it works' and it produces the vast wealth of the world today, is macho, bravado, and wrong. Capitalism works after a fashion, and has done so for thousands of years, but even today millions of people in the greatest capitalist nation on earth live lives of desperation, clearly denied the benefits of the system, while a few are spoiled by extravagant and undeserved rewards. In the rest of the world, the deprivation is even greater.

The political system which protects, absolutely, the private ownership of Capital requires a clear and concise philosophy   and name   if its benefits are to be made available to all; as well as securing the benefits for those already enjoying them. The terms 'free enterprise' or 'private enterprise' come closest to defining the system that we wish to describe. However, these again are more descriptions of the economic system rather than the political system. Historically, the name used was liberalism, but this term has been so hijacked by the socialists to designate welfare statism (*liberal* State hand-outs), that the term libertarianism has replaced it, and the old liberalism is now called classical liberalism. However, libertarianism has connotations of anarchism and so must be qualified as political libertarianism. We must admit, therefore, that there is, as yet, no proper term for the political system that completely protects the private ownership of Capital. Capitalism will still be used in spite of the overstretch of the word, and worse, because even the most 'capitalist' nations on earth have much Capital in the State's hands. Fuzzy thinking will continue to beget fuzzy thinking.

I hope this book will clear up the thinking about those elements of the political system which are essential in order to maximise the benefits of free enterprise. Then when the idea is more widely known, understood, and practised, someone somewhere will coin the correct term that encapsulates it precisely. Till then we will have to make do with this word 'capitalism'.

Freedom

Perhaps the greatest story told about freedom is that of a nation of slaves under the Egyptian Pharaoh escaping to found a new State, one that they felt gave them the freedoms they wanted. In modern times, we have seen the transformation that has occurred in the lives of millions of individuals from former communist States, many of which have now become prime movers in the free Western world structure. Poland and the Czech Republic in particular are very conscious of the importance of the freedoms won after such a long spell of communist oppression behind the Iron Curtain.

So what exactly defines Freedom? (A) Freedom of movement and association – we can go where we please and meet whom we please, plus (B) freedom to think and say what we like, in whatever media we like – we can express ourselves as we please. I believe that these two – freedom of movement and freedom of speech – are the two key ingredients in the concept of Freedom. We know, however, that freedoms are never absolute. Firstly, all freedoms are conditioned by the right of all others to the same freedoms, so our exercise of freedom cannot curb the freedom of our neighbour. Secondly, we live in a material world where most of our time is spent in working for our daily needs, so our freedom is not absolute, but we are largely free to choose the work that we do. So for the millions who suffered the hardships, restrictions and even prisons of the communists, these simple freedoms of movement and speech were the fresh air they longed for.

But even in the 'Free World', freedom is limited due to unemployment, poverty, and injustice. We should perhaps call it the 'relatively free world'. So what is missing? I suggest that the one thing still required to make Freedom complete is, Justice.

Justice

Long ago the concept of justice was perverted. In essence the concept is very simple: to give each their due. This is so simple, yet our minds are so bent by popular thought that we easily miss it. Taking it out of its normal context may make it easier to see what is meant by giving what is due. If someone takes great pleasure from a meal set before them, savouring every mouthful and cleaning every heaped plate the host provides, it can be said that the guest has done justice to the meal. The guest has given the meal the treatment that it deserved. Justice has been done.

To give each their due: so far removed have we become from this idea of justice that we hardly recognise it. We habitually think of justice as largely negative, where an offender is brought before the judge and given a punishment to fit the crime. This is our perverted view. Almost always the positive end of this form of justice is ignored: the injured or offended person rarely gets the restoration that is due to them. As long as the offender is punished, justice is said to be done. Little could be further from the truth. Yet the problem is even deeper.

To give each their due: the point at which Justice was perverted has vanished, lost in the distant past. Somehow, somewhere the idea was cut in two and it has died in the process. Economic justice became separated from criminal justice. What is due to someone for their work and effort has become a matter of economics, not of justice. Thus what an employee is paid becomes the least he/she is willing to accept in a bargain with an employer who is naturally seeking to maximise profit and who is also battling against economic injustice. This is institutionalised injustice on a grand scale which leads to so much of the poverty, want and unemployment that is so prevalent today. The deliberate theft of another's property

CHAPTER I • CAPITALISM, FREEDOM, JUSTICE AND THE MARKET 17

pales in comparison to this invisible theft, both are equally wrong but this economic theft is by far the more common and the bigger issue. We normally consider that you can only be robbed of what you already possess, but the non-payment of what is due to you is equally unjust. Perverted justice ignores the greater part of giving each their due.

But it gets still worse! So far have we departed from the concept that what a person earns is what he/she is due, that we actually have the reverse idea: a large portion of what is earned is due to others and must be removed by taxation. Envy, jealousy or just a desire to control may be the motives for this but such taxation has immunised us to the true concept of justice and we perceive this injustice as justice! Theft has become 'justice'! Justice has been well and truly perverted.

To give each their due: all States, governments, legislatures, councils and other public bodies need to be aware of this; revenue based on theft is injustice and will undo the good they aspire to. If they do not base their authority on justice but gain their power to act through injustice, they will undermine their own authority. Give what is due and take only what is just. In the chapter on taxation we will clarify how this can be achieved.

The enormous relief mankind will experience when we achieve the ideal of economic justice – where Labour and Capital receive their due reward – will transform the human psyche. The move from the present, where most people receive only a fraction of what they are due (breeding resentment and envy – subconscious and conscious), to the future righteousness of full reward for each individual input, will make man anew. Truly a new world awaits.

Justice is a simple concept: to give each their due. Very simple.

The free market

Champions of capitalism extol the virtues of the free market, and with good reason, for the free market is nothing more than free people offering their wares and purchasing their supplies out of their own free will and the necessities that nature places upon them. But there is a caveat: as discussed under freedom above, the so-called 'free market' is only partially free, and this is where the opponents of the market get their ammunition.

There is a saying that money is like water and finds its own level. Imagine a large basin filled with water an inch deep, with the level surface of the water representing the free market and the depth of water representing wealth / opportunity / prosperity. If the basin rests on a level surface, the opportunity / prosperity will be evenly distributed across the whole basin, but if we tilt one side of the basin up by one inch, on the surface the market looks completely free as before, but, when we examine the levels of opportunity / prosperity across the basin, there is a rich side and a poor side. If we (the State) then set up a series of pumps to suck water from the deep side and pump it across to the shallow side, we will quickly see that we make very little difference to the prevailing level of opportunity / prosperity, as the water rapidly reverts to level. Lots of energy is uselessly expended and the overall water level is actually reduced, while the otherwise still water is disturbed and distorted by turbulence; in fact this effort to correct a problem has only made matters worse. This illustrates the effect of State interference in the market today; it only makes matters worse. If we simply return the basin itself to level, then opportunity / prosperity is evenly distributed and the turbulence ceases.

The free market will never be truly free until it is also a just market with a level bottom as well as a level surface. The Georgist solution that we present later is the means whereby the basin may be returned to level, and a free and just market will result. The market is not Wall Street; the market is not Main Street; the market is free people trading on a level playing field. Nothing more, nothing less.

Land, Labour and Capital

Classical economists tell us that wealth is the product of three – and only three – factors of production, namely Land, Labour and Capital. The everyday usage of the first two terms are liable to throw us off the true meaning and value of this statement, while the meaning of the third is clouded by controversy, so we need to define each. For the sake of clarity, we will always use a capital letter for Land, Labour and Capital when they are used in the sense defined below.

Land

The term 'Land' as commonly used, applies to the dry surface of the earth and excludes bodies of water such as oceans, lakes and rivers. To the economist, however, these are included in the term Land: the Gulf of Mexico, the North Sea and the Caspian Sea as oil producing areas are wealth producing regions. Fishing 'grounds' are similarly aquatic sources of wealth. So when economists use the term 'Land' they are referring to 'natural resources', that is, what nature provides, to distinguish them from things that are produced by man's work. To the economist, 'Land' includes such intangible things as the radio spectrum which is a provision of nature through which so much economic traffic travels in our modern world. One day, we may have to include asteroids if they turn out to have commercial application. So 'Land' here includes all the natural resources that the universe provides us for free – it has no cost of production.

Labour

The term 'Labour' is commonly associated with the hard physical effort required to perform a task. However, in economics the term describes all physical and mental exertion used to produce goods or services, including all sorts of practices that are unlikely to build muscles or break sweat. So Labour includes entrepreneurial, managerial, professional and skilled work, as well as hard muscle work; the use of brain and brawn are both included in this term.

Capital

Capital, like capitalism, is a word loaded with many meanings and these have been the source of much confusion. Volumes have been written about it, some of which have divided the world in war, yet it is a term we are forced to use, just as we discovered with the term Capitalism above.

The term 'Capital' as used commonly, generally refers to any valuable asset, especially big ones, but when analysing the process of creating wealth, classical economics uses the term Capital to describe man-made elements as opposed to those provided by nature, Land. Capital is defined as man-made objects (tools) used in the creation of wealth. So for the purposes of this work we will keep this definition to explicitly differentiate between Land and Capital.

The real importance of this three factor model is the issue of *ownership* and thus the determination of entitlement to share the wealth produced. Individuals (Labour) own themselves and are directly entitled to their share called income or wages; Capital is man-made and so each unit has a traceable owner who is entitled to its share called interest or return on Capital. Land – the natural resources of the earth – is, however, the heritage of all and owned by none, so the distribution of its share is entirely different from the others; this we will discuss further in another chapter.

Everything then – absolutely everything – that goes into the creation of wealth and is the subject of economics may be classified under one of these three primary terms, Land, Labour or Capital. Each of these terms, of course, can be subdivided for more in-depth study, but the reverse is not possible. Neo-classical economics (the current standard global model) has destroyed sense and reason by suggesting that there are only two factors of production, Labour and Capital, thereby blinding the world to the wholesale theft operation conducted by the political elite and their cronies, thus condemning the world to regular, deep and protracted periods of economic failure. By including Land within Capital they cunningly deflect the question of private ownership of natural resources. A question we will address later.

CHAPTER 2

Origins of the State

'The best preparation for politics is the study of history.'
Polybus (200BC, Greek)

'Tyranny is always better organised than freedom.'
Charles Peguy (1873-1914, French)

INDIVIDUALS – and voluntary associations of individuals – occasionally infringe the liberty of other individuals, by accident or by design, the remedy for which may be found in the courts of justice. Such infringements are blots or stains upon society, but they do not represent a flaw in the structure of society. They are symptomatic of either the finite nature we inhabit or the moral flaw in individuals and they are to be expected in a free society. The only real threat that exists, or has ever existed, to the freedom of the individual and of free society, is the State itself.

From the beginning of civilization, the State has been used by those in power to maintain themselves at the expense of the freedom of the rest. Ancient Babylon did so for the King and his 'nobles', ancient Greece did it for the slave holders. Modern communism has done, and continues to do so for an elite intelligentsia/bureaucracy. That communism does it in the name of the people serves only to make it hypocritical as well as oppressive. Western democracies do it for an elite political speculative class. The Islamic State does it for a religious and gender elite. It is a curious fact that the only religion that considers itself unfulfilled without State power is Islam and it believes that it ultimately will be the supreme world power. The important issue for this book is that it is the power of the State that the elite seek, and which they use when they have obtained control. This only serves to highlight the problem inherent in State power, the problem which we are seeking to resolve.

If the only threat to the ultimate victory of individual freedom and free society is the State, then the question normally posed about how much individual freedom is possible, must be reversed: what are the maximum legitimate limits of the State? What are its proper functions in a free society? Only when the State is functioning within its strict limits will the powerhouse of capitalism be free to order the material affairs of mankind in the most benign and glorious way.

The State being the subject of our discussion, we would normally expect to begin with both a definition and an examination of its origin and history. But on both these counts we run into difficulties. The problem of definition arises because the overwhelming majority of objects and phenomena that we have experienced since becoming human have been either natural or man-made. Our brains are hard-wired to define any new thing as either natural or man-made, so anything that is the combination of both requires a new way of thinking, and this is not easy. The State, along with the market and money, are classic examples of human institutions which have evolved without specific planning, they are part natural and part man-made, forcing us to think outside the box.

The second problem – which probably stems from the above – is that the State means different things to different people and cultures. Louis XIV of France claimed that he was the State, *'L'Etat, c'est moi'*. In western democracies we tend to equate *elected* legislative and executive branches of government with the State. But this is neither the current nor the historical norm as most States have existed, and some continue to, without such elected bodies.

That said, the best definition of the State that I can find is: *'a body of people with a monopoly of power to enforce law within a certain geographical area'* (Max Webber, *Politics as a Vocation*, 1919). The key words here are *power, monopoly, force* and *law*; whether the 'body' is a despotic king or a democratically elected cabinet does not matter. Territory is important though it may change from time to time for any given State.[1]

---

[1] In English, the word 'state' is used in a number of different ways which may add to or subtract from our understanding of the term State. The word 'estate', meaning a large area of land, is clearly connected to our above definition and reinforces the concept of territory. The word 'statement' meaning a financial record, is pregnant with innuendo as the State has been since its inception a collector of money. The bulk of early writings are tax documents; records and receipts. Cuneiform script derives from this methodical record keeping. Indeed the famous Rosetta Stone is nothing more than one of many copies of a general proclamation of a tax amnesty by the →

Just as there exists no clear common understanding of the term State, the *origin* of the State as an historical entity is in dispute. The earliest *written* histories present us with State powers such as the ancient empires of Egypt, Babylon, Indus valley and China in their heyday – but this may be for no other reason than that the State was the cradle of writing as well as the other arts and sciences of civilization.

The earliest *archaeological* evidence of the existence of a State comes from the turn of the 4th to the 3rd Millennium BC (some 6,000 years ago) on the fertile plain between the Tigris and the Euphrates rivers, in modern Iraq. Here are found walled cities and clay fragments with the earliest forms of writing – cuneiform script. Here we learn of the existence of the city-States of Sumer and Lagash, but we can find no clue as to how they arose.

Since we cannot rely on historical / archaeological evidence to inform us directly of the primitive beginnings of the State, we will have to draw on many other branches of natural science, particularly anthropology, sociology and psychology, to see if we can construct a coherent theory of the origin of the State. *For if we can understand how the State arose, we may more easily understand why it is as it is today and, perhaps, grasp its essential nature.*

Two theories of the origin of the State

The best-known theory of the origin of the State is that which was first presented by Thomas Hobbes in the middle of the 1600s. This theory, called the Consensus Theory, was made popular by Jean Jacques Rousseau in *The Social Contract*, which he wrote in the 1750s. The theory holds that man in the savage state lived alone, initially coming together for breeding purposes only; then, in some mysterious way, uniting to agree to a 'social contract' – which presumably included a pact not to clobber each other! In this manner the first social organisation was formed, which in turn became the primordial 'State'. Thus man became civilised.

---

boy-king Ptolemy V, written in all the official languages of his empire. The word 'state' meaning circumstances at any time or a perturbed condition of mind may lead us to speculate as to the connection with the State - cause or effect - but does not provide us further help in our enquiry.

The problem with this theory is that it must first explain how the savages solved their Catch 22 situation – how to sit down for their parley on forming a social contract *without already having such a contract*. Indeed Rousseau simply assumes that a contract has been made somewhere in the past! Secondly, and more importantly, this theory must live up to two hundred years of scientific investigation into the origin of man which flatly denies that we were ever *solitary* animals.

Modern anthropology has revealed that Man was ever and always a *social* being, akin to the Gorilla and the Chimpanzee, making the Consensus Theory untenable if not actually laughable. And yet this is the thesis that has become dominant among social scientists of today. Surprising as this may seem at first sight, the reason why is not too difficult to find: the Consensus (or social contract) Theory is politically cosy; it says that we have the present system because we have – in the past – agreed to it, so there is no need to question the status quo. Those who hold political power finance the sciences, and they do not want anyone to rock their luxury cruise liner!

The rival 'Conflict Theory' is politically unpopular because it asks awkward questions of those 'in power'[2]. It is, however, far more credible as a scientific thesis, and it bears the hallmark of all good ones. It explains many, otherwise unexplained phenomena such as national feeling, class separation, and party politics.

The Conflict Theory of the origin of the State has been around for some time. The historian Alexander Rustow, in *Freedom and Domination*, traces the history of the theory (the 'superstratification hypothesis' in Rustow's terminology) to the Arab sociologist Ibn Khaldun, 1332-1406 (Rustow, Alexander, *Freedom and Domination*, Princeton University Press, 1980, p.5) and finds it evident in the works of many other writers. Rustow was introduced to the idea by Franz Oppenheimer whose book *The State* (German edition, 1908) contains the most succinct exposition of the thesis. For this reason, and because this theory is so little known, yet so pertinent, we will outline Oppenheimer's work below.

Franz Oppenheimer was born in Berlin on 30th March 1864, the son of a Rabbi, and, having practised medicine for a decade returned to study, receiving his Ph.D. at Kiel at the age of 44. In 1933 he left Germany and taught in France and Palestine; in 1938 he went to Japan and then to the U.S.A. He died in Los Angeles on 30th September 1943.

---

[2] The phrase "in power" is itself good linguistic evidence for the Conflict Thesis.

Oppenheimer begins his thesis of the origin of the State by noting that the material necessities of life make the satisfaction of economic need the primary requirement of man. Then he notes that there are two – and only two – means of satisfying economic need: 1. Labour and 2. Robbery.

In the early stages of human tribal existence, robbery was not a reliable route for the satisfaction of material requirements as storable surpluses had not yet developed. Once agricultural technology had developed sufficiently to produce storable surpluses, the option for a stronger tribe to live by robbing the stores of weaker tribes became a temptation. Where robbery had initially been practised

Franz Oppenheimer, originator of the Conflict Theory of the Origin of the State, Germany/U.S.A., 1864-1943.
Original in Central Zionist Archive, Jerusalem.

only on an individual or sporadic scale, now it could be the source of livelihood for a whole tribe, indeed it could become so much a way of life that the tribe of robbers could live by this means alone, and their previous labours could be abandoned or practised only for pleasure.

Oppenheimer then discusses the different types of tribal peoples found in history (peoples without a State) and notes that the relative equality or inequality within a tribe is conditioned by their means of sustenance. Only in the tribes where strict organisation is a prerequisite to economic gain – in the herding and fishing peoples – is differentiation into classes possible. In hunter-gatherer communities and tiller peoples this differentiation does not happen because of the ease with which a family or clan may move to another site without material loss, avoiding oppression by other members of the tribe.

In the herding and fishing peoples, however, the *tense discipline* (required for successful herding and seagoing) forces strict organisation within the tribe. Here the *culture* of statehood is formed but the *substance* is lacking. Slaves and freemen can still flee or rebel with comparative ease; the chief who becomes intolerable may still be ousted.

At this stage of State formation, where tribes constantly rub shoulders and friction occurs, the herding and fishing tribes have an immediate advantage over hunter-gatherers and tillers: transport. Pack animals or mounts in the form of horses and camels are the tools of the trade for herding people, while sea-worthy vessels serve the fishing people. Transport means speed of attack, and retreat, as well as ability to carry away goods and humans. Fighting *between* herding/fishing peoples carries roughly equal chances of win or lose, but for either of these tribes against the hunter-gatherers the odds improve, but against the tillers the chance of success approaches certainty.

Of the hunter-gatherers and the tillers, the former only hunt or gather enough for immediate or imminent use, and so are not useful targets for the herders or fishers to attack. The tillers are a different matter. Tilling peoples have a strictly limited set of harvest times when food is in great surplus and thus they become 'honey-pots' for the robber tribes. Furthermore, tillers lack the killer instinct of the hunters making them softer targets.

Thus the raiding of the herder or fisher peoples against the tillers becomes an established historical fact in which Oppenheimer sees the first stage of true State development.[3] The oppression of one group of people by another – which has characterised the history of States universally – begins here.

Stage one

This may last for thousands of years and may never develop further, it simply remains the story of the area, the raids become predictable and regular, accompanied by killing and destruction. Oppenheimer likens this stage to the bear that destroys the hive to feast on the honey, enough bees may survive to re-establish themselves, but they may equally die out as a result of the raid.

Stage two

Where circumstances are ripe, the raiders come to understand that if they loot only the surplus and do not kill or damage the subject[4] tribe then it

---

[3] Where there are no domesticable herds and hence no herders (such as in ancient Mexico) it is the Hunters who became the raiders and thus the rulers of the embryo State.

will recover more quickly and be in a position of surplus again sooner. The raiders come as before but use violence only to enforce respect and take only the surplus. The wanton killing of a subject becomes a crime within the raider tribe. The bear has turned beekeeper. This step is beneficial to both the raiders and the victims. This is evolutionary in the sense that this situation will tend to survive and flourish compared with stage one.

Stage three

But the new consciousness of the beekeeper quickly leads to a third stage where the raider tribe desires to protect its subject tribe from the raids of other bears or beekeepers, and so defends its subject tribe from all other attackers. In return the subject tribe may desire – or be forced – to bring the booty, renamed tribute, to their masters.

Stage four

Once again stage three contains 'evolutionary advantage' and quickly leads to the fourth stage, where the raiders move their base camp close to, or inside, the lands of the tillers. Protection of the subjects is made easier and the raiders may now have given up all effort to maintain themselves by their own work and commit themselves solely to increasing the number of tribes under their subjection. Natural selection works again: the beekeepers extend *their* territory and increase the number of subject tribes: empire is born.

Stage five

Soon a fifth stage becomes necessary where the raiders feel obliged to keep order among their flourishing subjects and for the first time raiders become rulers.

Stage six

The sixth stage, which is the completion of the primitive State, is reached when the rulers habitually judge the disputes of the subjects, and they direct their subject's activities in a premeditated manner. Increasing the size of the harvest now becomes the concern of the rulers, while survival becomes the concern of the subject. Modern history and civilization are born.

---

[4] Further linguistic evidence for the truth of the Conflict Thesis: even today, U.K. citizens are still called 'subjects' of the monarch.

Oppenheimer emphasises that these stages are not necessarily completed for each State as it developed, but are conceptual tools useful to examine 'Statefulness' of differing tribal situations. To recap, the stages of 'Statefulness' are:

1 Tribal robbery accompanied by killing and destruction.
2 The robbery persisting but killing and destruction are seen to be counterproductive and they cease.
3 The subject tribe brings 'tribute' to their conquering tribe in exchange for defence against other conquering tribes.
4 Territorial union of the two tribes or garrisons of 'protection' formed. Territorial expansion.
5 Conquerors keep 'order' among subject peoples.
6 Habit of rule and usage of government.

This is the Conflict Theory of the origin of the State. Is this how States really emerged or was it by the consensus route? Oppenheimer admits that some States may well have originated by consensus and he gives the U.S.A and Switzerland as examples, but he strenuously asserts that, as an entity the State is '...a social institution, forced by a victorious group of men on a defeated group, with the sole purpose of regulating the dominion of the victorious group over the vanquished, and securing itself against revolt from within and attacks from abroad ... this dominion had no other purpose than the economic exploitation of the vanquished by the victors.'

While much has changed from Stage Six – the primitive State – to our modern constitutional State, much remains the same. The oppressive nature of taxation is readily apparent, as are the desire of rulers to direct and control the economy, to increase territory by war or treaty, and to cling to power for as long as possible. Power is still control by the few, and subjection is still degradation and frustration for the many.

The State, though the cradle of civilization, is birthed in economic exploitation and has settled into maturity wrapped in this foetal sack. And until this realisation becomes accepted wisdom, man will not be able to free himself to be as he should; he is doomed to kow-tow to the State and be moulded in its image. As long as the Conflict Theory of the origin of the State remains obscure, man will lack the tools to forge for himself the true freedom which remains his heart's desire. As long as we continue to view the State as the provider of all that is good and that we are its voluntary subjects, so long will we be fettered by it. If we are unaware of the truth about the origin of the State we will remain powerless to undo the damage that it is causing.

Oppenheimer's theory explains much that has so far been unsatisfactorily explained or not at all. The uneasy coalition of rulers and ruled that has survived into modern democratic States is now easily understood: the feeling in politics of 'them' and 'us', and of the hopelessness of the bulk of citizens (subjects) in achieving change, is understandable. Indeed the whole history of States since feudal times becomes comprehensible in the light of this thesis. The conflict between States is seen as the conflict between rulers – for more subjects and territories: a hundred years ago World War I was a fight between siblings and cousins in the ruling clans of Europe.

The conflict between subjects and rulers that has characterised the internal history of States also becomes clear; the class war that has been roused by socialist doctrines is both understandable and can now be seen to be heading in the wrong direction. *It is irrelevant who holds power, the problem lies in the exploitative nature of the State itself. It removes power from individuals through taxation, transferring it to the State treasury, where it is gamed by the political elite.*

Political parties and the parliamentary principle of 'opposition' can be seen as deriving from the representatives of both the subjects and the rulers, who constantly trade periods of 'being in power'. This phrase 'in power' which has become (through repetitive and glib use) meaningless, now springs to life in terrifying revelation of the truth: power robbed from the many is given over to the few.

The conflict within nation-States has largely been transformed into heated political exchanges and avoids the shedding of blood. Though there continue to be many minor conflicts all over the world which we now call guerrilla warfare or insurgency, it is still war. Some States continue to single out one section of the population (a tribe) for genocide as the Nazi Germans did of the Jews, and the Stalinist regime did to the Land-tied peasants of parts of the Russian Empire, and as the Arab rulers of Sudan do to the native tribes today.

The task ahead is to refine those parts of the State concept that are beneficial, and to remove those that are intrinsically exploitative, those hangovers of the conflicts that initiated the State in the first place.

Nothing in the Conflict Theory denies the possibility that voluntary contracts took place both in the pre-State tribal situation, and within the State structure, but the whole point is *that it is the monopolisation of force which is the defining feature of the State.* At the same time we can see that the genesis of all human conflicts – including State conflicts – lies in the evil that exists in the heart of individuals. And therein lies the transcendent wisdom of faith that points to individual transformation as the cure for society. This individual transformation must continue even as we press forward with correct political measures; both the transcendent and the immanent are necessary. We will discuss this further in Chapter 9.

*

We began with a definition of the State as *'a body of people with a monopoly of power to enforce law within a certain territorial area'*, and we have examined the merits of the little known Conflict Theory of its origin, showing it to have very strong internal cohesion even if we have been unable to prove it was the origin of the State. Perhaps it is impossible ever to prove which theory of the State's origin is the correct one, but we have shown that there is a perfectly plausible alternative to the Consensus Theory and that we cannot simply accept the latter without question. If the Conflict Theory is unproven so also is the Consensus Theory.

If we examine the above definition of the State, we can note the following:

1   'a body of people' translates into 'a ruling body';
2   'a monopoly of power' translates into 'a military force';
3   'enforcing law' translates into 'police and taxation';
4   'territory' remains 'territory'.

These four things are common to all States in history everywhere and hold equally true today. However, there are so many areas of life in which the State has involved itself, that in certain situations, such as communism, it would be easier to list the functions of the individual than the functions of the State. This is, however, the very problem that we set out to solve: what are the legitimate functions of the State? So if natural science can give a definition of the State that is satisfactory, but cannot achieve the same agreement on the origin and essential nature of the State, we must dig even deeper to find the key to understanding. We must enter the realm of Philosophy and natural Law.

CHAPTER 3

Natural Law

'Natural law is so immutable that God himself could not change it.'
Hugo Grotius (Dutch Jurist, 1583-1645)

'Economics has its own laws which are just as terrible to violate
as the laws of the atomic reactor in Chernobyl.'
Nikolay Shmelyov (Russian Economist, 1936-2014)

T HE STUDY of natural science in any of its fields – physics, chemistry, biology, geology, etc. – reveals certain patterns in nature, and these patterns have been termed 'Laws'.[5] These Laws extend (as far as they are testable) throughout nature, from the level of the sub-atomic, as far as the speed of light. The whole material universe, including the material aspects of human existence, runs according to Law. We must all eat to stay alive – this is a natural Law. We may speculate on nature outside the known boundaries, but as long as we exist in the flesh we live within these Laws and cannot break them.

The sciences of physiology, psychology and sociology constantly attest to the patterns that run through human existence; we have free will, to be sure, but it is freedom under natural Law. We *must* eat, but we are free to choose what we eat. Our bodies *cannot* fly, but we are free to use the Laws of physics to construct flying machines that can carry us, etc., etc. Our freedom is vast but it is not absolute – indeed no-one ever said it was.

---

[5] In this book, Law spelt with a capital denotes that it is natural; law spelt in the lower case denotes civil or State authority.

31

The discovery of these natural Laws has been of incomparable benefit to the human race, for they have allowed us to adjust our activities to make the best use of our energies in securing improved conditions for our material existence. The passing of electric current through Tungsten filaments gives us light; compressing gas will raise its temperature while decompressing it will cool it, giving us refrigeration and air conditioning. Such Laws are also apparent (to those who will look) in the science of economics, dealing as it does with the activities of people and the creation of wealth. However, the problem is that, since economics involves wealth and thus power, members of any power monopoly will use that power to thwart any attempt at revealing and implementing such Laws. For if the Laws of economics were known and fully understood, the power monopoly would be broken and those individuals would be deprived of their privileges. As we have seen, the Conflict Theory of the origin of the State holds that rulers do indeed have such a power monopoly, which explains why these natural Laws of economics continue to be ignored.

Man, however, has free will and may in any particular case behave contrary to any Law, if he is so determined and is enabled to do so by *a different Law*, but this does not deny the existence of the Law that was not followed. For example, a man may choose to fast till he dies, but his action does not negate the basic Law that humans are living creatures who need to eat.

Here we encounter an important aspect of natural Law, namely that there is a hierarchy of Laws with some Laws being more all-embracing than others. For example, the Law of Gravity is fundamental to all activity on the Earth's surface, but the application of the Laws of Aerodynamics will lift birds and aeroplanes in opposition to gravity. These cases, which appear to contravene the Law of Gravity, illustrate how one particular law may in specific circumstances set aside a more general Law, but this can only be temporary – eventually the more fundamental Law will triumph. Birds, aeroplanes and even satellites will succumb to gravity sooner or later.

Similarly, on Earth everything appears to grind to a halt if energy is not applied to keep them in motion; we might call this the Law of Stasis. Freed from the earth's gravitational pull, however, we note the opposite is true: Objects will continue in constant motion without end. This is a superior natural Law, the Law of the Conservation of Momentum.

So we see that there exists a hierarchy of natural Laws, where one may temporarily be overridden by harnessing another. Ultimately there is the struggle of Life, which tends to organise matter, and Entropy, where matter tends to disintegrate. The resolution of this process is highly speculative and may involve Laws and realms of which we are barely aware, but its relevance to this discussion lies in the fact that Life allows free will. Man, using this free will, may choose temporarily to follow a less fundamental Law, but in the end the more fundamental Law *will* be followed, willy-nilly. It is the fundamental natural Law of the State which we seek, so that we may follow *it* and not any contrived man-made law.

Law in economics

The first Law of Economics, as formulated by both Frederic Bastiat and Henry George, whom we will meet shortly, is '*man always seeks to meet his needs with the least possible exertion*'. Here we can see a clear parallel with a couple of the Laws of Physics: the Conservation of Momentum and the Conservation of Energy. Indeed we can almost say that the first Law of Economics is an expression of the Conservation of Energy Law in an economic context. We could call it 'The Law of Minimum Exertion', from which stems all the inventiveness and cooperation of humankind in the procurement of our needs from nature, but, as we have seen, this has also been the motive force behind the plundering raids of the first State-forming enterprises and the continuation of plunder down the ages – '*man always seeks to meet his needs with the least possible exertion.*' It ain't just the teenager, it's a natural Law!

Natural Law operates within the whole field of human activity, but because we are so close to this activity we frequently 'cannot see the wood for the trees' and we fail to see that these Laws apply. We have failed for such a long time even to see these Laws that we have come to think that they do not exist. The natural Laws of human activity are largely denied by those who should know better. But we may console ourselves because the same thing happened when the Law of Conservation of Momentum was being formulated: on an apparently flat earth it seemed that things generally ground to a halt, however, when gravity and the curvature of the earth were accepted, then the Law of Conservation of Momentum could be seen. Only when we rise above the situation (so to speak) can we see the underlying Laws that govern it.

Law in psychology

Certain natural Laws in the field of human behaviour are well understood and established in everyday language, even if not consciously termed Laws. One such Law is 'incentive'; when offered a reward people will *tend* to do what is desired. Threatened by fines, people will *tend* to avoid that which is forbidden. We are here talking of tendencies, or patterns, or Laws. Just because we have freedom of will, and we may choose to tread a different path, this does not negate the fact that these patterns are in fact Laws. We are familiar with the phrase 'all else being equal' used to qualify a statement about such tendencies, and with this qualifier we may call certain patterns of human behaviour – Laws.

A good example of this is found in the recognition by the State of the usefulness of the 'Law of Incentive' when it applies the penalty of fines to activities it wants to discourage, such as the speeding of vehicles on the roads. The very same organisation has been mighty slow, however, to see that the same Law operates through the taxes it imposes on the work, production and consumption which it professes to encourage. So slow has it been that one suspects it does not *want* to see this effect; it wishes to remain blind to this fact. Never-the-less, that Law is there and its effects are real, and when it is eventually recognised, revenue may be raised in accordance with it. This will encourage harmony and symbiosis in human material existence, and will lead to the ironing out of much of the discord in human society.

Natural Law in legislated and constitutional law

We have so far observed natural Law existing throughout nature, including human activities; we should therefore not be too surprised to find that it also exists in the constitution and affairs of the State. But, as we have noted above, any privileged ruling group is likely to thwart the spreading of the knowledge of the natural Law which governs the relationship of ruler and ruled and which, if effected, would undermine the ruler's privilege.[6] A natural Law of the State has indeed been

---

[6] The word 'privilege' comes from the Latin for private law, *privus-legis*, and is further linguistic evidence for the Conflict Theory of the Origin of the State. For how could a private law come out of a 'social contract'?

formulated by two great men quite independently, but their fate has been the same: their formulations have been ignored and their names almost forgotten.

The first of these men, Frederic Bastiat, was born in June 1801 in the southwest of France, in the small provincial town of Bayonne overlooking the Bay of Biscay and overshadowed by the Pyrenean mountains. Having spent most of his life in leisurely study and farming, Bastiat was drawn, by the convulsions of the French State, into journalism and debate; and eventually, by the Revolution of 1848,

Frederic Bastiat, originator of the Law of the State, France, 1801-1850.

into becoming an elected representative of the National Assembly of the Second French Republic. He died in Rome on Christmas eve 1850, having written the major treatises by which he is remembered in his last few years. The unashamed violence and bloodshed of the period led Bastiat to conceive the most rigorous protection possible against its recurrence. The modern mind may shrink from the conclusions that Bastiat has drawn, but the power of his logic is inescapable and we ignore him at our peril.

The second formulator of the Law of the State was Herbert Spencer who was born in April 1820 in Derby, England and died in December 1903 in Brighton. Spencer is generally a better known thinker and philosopher whose authorship was prodigious, and in virtually all his work there runs a thin but consistent thread of natural Law. He was a complicated being and we encounter a problem when discussing his ideas as he completely reversed a section of them in mid-career. Indeed he became a champion of the opposition to the very ideas he had formerly proposed; we must therefore speak of the early- or late-Spencer. The 1851 edition of *Social Statics* (which belongs to his early work) comes to virtually the same conclusion as Bastiat. Since the two men were writing at the same time but hundreds of miles apart without the connectivity of the phone or even the telegraph, it is unlikely that either one was influenced in his thought by the other. Spencer, however, draws out a function of the State which neither Bastiat nor anyone else has put forward. We will return to this point later.

The Law of the State – as with all good formulations of scientific Law – is exceedingly simple, and like many has been ignored. Newton's Law of Conservation of Momentum came to be generally accepted only when it was found that, applied to particular examples, it accurately predicted the outcomes. But this acceptance did not occur immediately; reactionary and disbelieving forces had to be overcome first. Similarly the Laws of Planetary Rotation, formulated by Galileo and Copernicus were resisted by a massive vested interest. The Church at the time clung to the belief that the Earth was the centre of the universe and it used its great powers in a most diabolical manner to stifle the new thinking. It took a long time before the Laws of Planetary Rotation were generally accepted.

The principle that underlies the State will undermine – in the same fashion as the principles of planetary rotation – the power base of those in authority. Recognition of it will therefore be thwarted or ignored as long as possible; the powers-that-be have so far succeeded for 150 years to the extent that Bastiat and Spencer's ideas on this issue have been consigned to the intellectual fringe.

The Law of the State

The principle, or Law, may be derived like this: the enforcement of the laws of a State *necessarily* involves the use of force, or the threat of it, against persons. Without the use or threat of force, the State cannot function. And since the State is a human institution, and as people are bound by moral Laws, *the State may do only those things that are **legitimately** performed by force*. This is the Law of the State.

Or we may also look at it this way: Nature provides that all organisms (outside of humans) have natural rights. That is to say that each organism may freely exercise its power to sustain itself, using force wherever necessary. Humans too have this natural right, to use force against other organisms, including other humans. But this right is refined a couple of stages under the State, by (A) combining the common right into one body (the State) and (B) limiting the right to use force on other humans to self-defence. This combining and limiting of the natural right to use force, carried to its logical conclusion arrives at the same destination. The natural Law of the State then, as formulated by Bastiat and the early Spencer, is this: *'The State may do* only *those things that are legitimately performed by force' and nothing else.*

The Law of the State is the Law of legitimate force

Bastiat made no comment on the origin of the State as an entity, he saw what existed and made his own deductions. His insight into the essential nature of the State is so logical, clear and original that it is worth quoting two pages from his best-selling essay 'The Law'. First published as a pamphlet in June 1850, this book has been translated[7] into English more than once, and has sold over a million copies.

Beginning with the note that our lives and the natural resources of the earth are given to us by God, our creator, Bastiat goes on:

> By the application of our faculties to these natural resources we convert them into products and use them. This process is necessary in order that life may run its appointed course.
>
> Life, faculties, production – in other words, individuality, liberty, property – this is man ... And these three gifts from God precede all human legislation, and are superior to it.
>
> Life, liberty and property do not exist because men have made laws. On the contrary, it was the fact that life, liberty and property existed beforehand that caused men to make laws in the first place.
>
> Each of us has a natural right ... to defend his person, his liberty, and his property ... it follows that a group of men have the right to organise and support a common force to protect these rights constantly. Thus the principle of collective right – its reason for existing, its legitimacy – is based on individual right. And the common force that protects this collective right cannot logically have any other purpose or any other mission than that for which it acts as a substitute. Thus since an individual cannot legitimately use force against the person, liberty or property of another individual, then the common force – for the same reason – cannot be used to destroy the person, liberty or property of individuals or groups.
>
> The law is the organisation of the natural right of legitimate defence. It is the substitution of a common force for individual forces. And this

---

[7] I am using Dean Russell's 1950 translation, with the sole exception of the word '*legitime*' where I follow Seymour Cain 1964 in rendering it 'legitimate', whereas Russell has it as 'lawful'.

common force is to do only what the individual forces have a natural and legitimate right to do: to protect persons, liberties and properties; to maintain the right of each, and to cause justice to reign over us all.

And in all sincerity can anything more than the absence of plunder be required of the law? Can the law – which necessarily requires the use of force – rationally be used for anything except protecting the rights of everyone? I defy anyone to extend it beyond this purpose without perverting it, and, consequentially, turning might against right. This is the most fatal and most illogical social perversion that can possibly be imagined. It must be admitted that the true solution – so long searched for in the area of social relationships – is contained in these simple words: law is organised justice.

Now this must be said: When justice is organised by law – that is, by force – it excludes the idea of using law (force) to organise any human activity whatever, whether it be labour, charity, agriculture, commerce, industry, education, art or religion. The organising by law of any one of these would inevitably destroy the essential organisation – justice. For truly, how can we imagine force being used against the liberty of citizens without it also being used against justice, and thus acting against its proper purpose? ...

Since the law organises justice, the socialists ask why the law should not be used for these purposes? Because it could not organise labour, education, and religion without destroying justice. We must remember that law is force, and that, consequentially, the proper functions of the law cannot legitimately extend beyond the proper functions of force.

When law and force keep a person within the bounds of justice, they impose nothing but a mere negation. They violate neither his personality, his liberty, nor his property. They safeguard all of these. They are defensive; they defend equally the rights of all.

As a friend of mine once remarked, this negative concept of law is so true that the statement, *the purpose of the law is to cause justice to reign*, is not a rigorously accurate statement. It ought to be stated that *the purpose of the law is to prevent injustice from reigning*. In fact, it is injustice, instead of justice, that has an existence of its own. Justice is achieved only when injustice is absent.

But when the law, by means of its necessary agent, force, imposes upon men a regulation of labour, a method or a subject of education, a religious faith or creed – then the law is no longer negative; it acts positively upon people. It substitutes the will of the legislator for their own wills; the initiative of the legislator for their own initiatives. When this happens, the people no longer need to discuss, to compare, to plan ahead; the law does all this for them. Intelligence becomes a useless prop for the people; they cease to be men; they lose their personality, their liberty, their property.

Try to imagine a regulation of labour imposed by force that is not a violation of liberty; a transfer of wealth imposed by force that is not a violation of property. If you cannot reconcile these contradictions, then you must conclude that the law cannot organise labour and industry without organising injustice.

There it is! Simple and incontrovertible. *The force of law can only be legitimately derived from the natural right of individuals to self-defence.* Therefore this is the limit of the law – to defend the citizen. Whether the State originated in a legitimate manner (by consensus) or illegitimately (by conflict) is not the important point; it must simply conform its operations to natural Law. It must *become* legitimate.

This conclusion – of both Bastiat and Spencer – that government should be involved only with the administration of justice through its monopoly of force is shocking to most people. Somehow the feeling arises that affairs of State cannot be so simple. How will everything else function? So used are we to the powerful and proactive nature of the State that we can hardly imagine such a limited State – the Minimal State. Yet it stares us in the face and confronts us with its perfect logic. If we conceive of any further function for the State we conceive injustice – we procreate evil. Force may only be used on people to remove injustice. Period!

This natural Law – the Law of Legitimate Force – that the State may do only that which is legitimately performed by force, is a simple and powerful formula. Here at last we have dug deep enough to secure the foundations of a truly free society – *the State may have no other function outside of administering Justice.*

> The law of the State is the Law of Legitimate Force. The State may perform only those functions where the use of force is legitimate.

Though this formula has largely been ignored for the one hundred and fifty years since Bastiat, Libertarians have continued to champion the idea and kept it alive, and for that we can be grateful. Unfortunately, however, Libertarians have not addressed themselves to the question of how the State may be funded in a way that *is itself* a means of promoting justice. They have either skipped over the problem or fudged it. This will be the subject for the next chapter.

*

The intellectual insecurity of capitalism and the free world did not prevent its victory in the long struggle with communism that dominated the

20th century. This insecurity does, however, leave capitalism and freedom prey for any of the socialist/totalitarian perversions which still roam intellectual elite circles undefeated. The stupendous loss of innocent life under these regimes in the past, such as Mao, Stalin and Hitler etc. should spur us on to shore up capitalism/freedom's intellectual defences so that the world may never see such bloodshed again. Nor is it just about loss of life; few under such regimes actually live any kind of quality of life at all. An errant smile or word can put the subject of such a State in a gulag. Freedom is about living *'life to the full'*, and this is what we want to secure.

In our effort so far we began by examining both the origins of the State and what defines a State, but neither led us to discover the principles that underlie it.

Lastly we have delved into the theory of natural Law, and noting that all things – including the State – are governed by natural Laws, we eventually reached the conclusion of Bastiat, that the Law of the State is the Law of Legitimate Force. Here at last we located the foundation for the philosophy of freedom. With this understanding we have solid ground on which to build. Now we can explore what this means for the various branches of the State and what its shape will be; these will be the topics for the following chapters.

PART II

The Three Proposals

CHAPTER 4

Raising Revenue without Taxation

'The power to tax is the power to destroy.'
John Marshall
(U.S. Supreme Court Chief Justice, 1755-1835)

'To tax and to be loved is not given to man.'
Queen Elizabeth I, 1533-1603

T HE FIRST NEED of any State, whatever its origin, size or political hue, is to raise revenue in order to maintain itself and carry out its functions. Just as Oppenheimer noted that the material necessities for the sustenance of life make the satisfaction of economic needs the *primary* requirement of the individual, so also the same idea holds for the State. And revenue has traditionally meant that old bugbear – taxation.

The Libertarians who have championed the Minimal State have usually tackled the problem of taxation by proposing that either the State is some sort of voluntary organisation subscribed to by enough individuals to make it work (Robert Nozick: *Anarchy, State and Utopia*). Or that it is run by democratically elected representatives whose choice of taxes is – precisely because those who decide are *democratically* elected – perfectly just (The Foundation for Economic Education and The Providence Foundation).

Neither of these approaches address the central point – the State must only administer justice. In other words, the very means of raising revenue must itself be just. The first method above approaches this by making subscription to the State voluntary; but there is little to suggest that this might work in practice and much that says it would not. The problem of free riders makes it unfair to those who do subscribe, so it would be essentially unjust.

The second approach is simply a cop out. The present system of taxation is to be left largely intact, and therein lies the problem: most of the present taxes have derived from oppression and injustice, and they remain oppressive and unjust. They cannot be left as they are. Indeed, as we have seen from Oppenheimer's analysis of the origin of the State, taxation – as the direct descendant of booty and tribute – *is probably the greatest source of injustice that exists today*, and it has done untold damage throughout history. Taxation itself must be removed.

The great interest aroused by the announcement of the budget in any democratic country is one indication of the importance of this topic, while the continuous attempts to avoid and evade taxes show how it fills many lives in the effort to get around it. An authority in this field, Charles Montesquieu (1689-1755) writing in *The Spirit of the Laws*, Book XI, Section 6 states: *'the raising of public money ... [is] ... the most important point of legislation.'*

It follows that the funding of government must be the first of its functions to be harmonised with natural Law. For if revenue is raised in ways that cut across the (natural) Laws of Economics and Psychology, then many problems will be induced, which – no matter what further 'positive' legislation is enacted and enforced – will never be eradicated. In fact this has been precisely what many centuries of legislation have attempted to do; but since more revenue is required to fund such legislated activity, it has been as fruitful as trying to lift oneself by one's bootlaces – the harder one tries the more energy is uselessly expended. It leads only to exhaustion, broken backs and bootlaces – and deeply indebted governments.

No matter how large or small the revenue required for the proper functioning of the State, it must all be raised in accordance with justice and natural Law. This we must first examine. Here we are dealing with money, wealth and property, so we need to investigate the rights involved with them. What are the rights of the individual and the State in regard to property? The answer to this question will guide us as to how the State may raise its own revenue.

The most famous and most quoted work on the theory of property rights comes from John Locke. He was born 29th August 1632 at Wrington, near Bristol, and having studied at Christ Church, Oxford, he was patronised by the Earl of Shaftesbury, continuing his study and writing. As a radical Christian he followed his patron into five and a half years of religious exile in Holland from 1683. On his return in 1689 he published *The Second Treatise on Civil Government*. He died on 28th October 1704 in Essex.

In his *Treatise*, Locke asserts that, because all men have '*property*' in their own '*persons*', it follows that the Labour of their bodies and the work of their hands are theirs also; this against the backdrop of: '*the earth and all inferior creatures be common to all men*'.

John Locke, originator of the Law of Property, England, 1632-1704.
© Bettmann/CORBIS

Whatsoever, then, he removes out of the state that Nature hath provided and left it in, he hath mixed his labour with it, and joined to it something that is his own, and thereby makes it his property. It being by him removed from the common state Nature placed it in, it hath by this labour something annexed to it that excludes the common right of other men. For this 'labour' being the unquestionable property of the labourer, no man but he can have a right to what that is once joined to, at least where there is enough, and as good left in common for others.

The Second Treatise on Civil Government,
Chapter V, Section 26

John Locke's essential point is that when someone applies their Labour to something, that thing, having been common property, now becomes the property of the individual whose Labour has been invested in it. Locke does not make a distinction between objects separate from the planet and those that remain intrinsically attached. In the first case there can be no objection to his thesis, the labourer becomes the sole owner of that object. 100%, period!

In the case of 'real estate' property, objections to Locke's thesis may be quickly found and we may conjecture that that is why he penned the proviso of the last sentence quoted above, '… *at least where there is enough, and as good left in common for others'*. However, this proviso may easily be rendered meaningless, as Nozick in *Anarchy, State and Utopia*, amply demonstrates. Chapter 7, Section 1:

> Consider the first person Z for whom there is not enough and as good left to appropriate. The last person Y to appropriate left Z without his previous liberty to act and so worsened Z's situation. So Y's appropriation is not allowed under Locke's proviso. Therefore the next to last person, X, to appropriate, left Y in a worse position, for X's act ended permissible appropriation. Therefore X's appropriation wasn't permissible. But then the appropriator two from last, W, ended permissible appropriation, and so, since it worsened X's position, W's appropriation wasn't permissible. And so on to the first person A to appropriate a permanent property right.

While Locke's proposition holds completely true for the products of Labour, it cannot be called upon to support the private ownership of Land. Since Land cannot – by definition – be made, it cannot be subject to the same natural Law of ownership that moveable goods are. The problem is that much Labour remains attached to Land – in the form of buildings, mine shafts, wells, Land improvements, and crops pre-harvest – and these all must be protected as fully and as firmly as movable property. Most commonly this protection has been effected by extending in full the notion of private property to include Land. This is, however, a very blunt instrument which in no way takes account of the common rights of all to Land. Fortunately a more subtle and fair system exists which firmly protects the labourer's investments attaching to the Earth while at the same time protecting the common rights of everyone else in the Land.

Locke's essential point, that the *origin* of Property Rights is found in Labour, and that the labourer is the full owner of all that he produces, follows his statement that *'the earth and all inferior creatures be common to all men'*. And this is the heart of the issue – *the Earth is common property*. Almost all Lockeans miss this point!

In order to establish secure title to the product of Labour when it is attached to Land, *outright* ownership of the Land is not necessary, and it is in fact excluded by Locke's foundational remark – Land is common property. It is the *unqualified* nature of the ownership of Land which is unsustainable and inconsistent with any theory of individual rights or equity. This simply means that property rights in Land (natural resources) must be *qualified*, and this may be achieved as follows: 'ownership' of Land is justified through regular payments by the 'owner' of a regular – probably monthly – fee (rent or tax) to the community, for exclusive rights to that site. In this way the right of private property in the products of Labour is protected, while the common ownership of Land is upheld. Equity is restored.

In *Social Statics* (Chapter X, 'The Right of Property', paragraph 3), Herbert Spencer reinforces this point further saying that *only when* a system of Land ownership which respects the rights of all is established, does the right of private property in the product of Labour hold true. In other words, the right of private property in the product of Labour *depends* on the common right of all to the earth being upheld.

Once this natural Law of property is understood, it becomes clear that the appropriation of anyone's property in the form of taxes on income, value added, profits, Capital etc., amounts to theft. And theft by the State is as immoral and as damaging as that perpetrated by any private person or gang, and must be ended.

On the other hand, the requirement of equal rights for everyone to Land provides the State with a tailor-made supply of funds for its needs. By levying a 'tax' on the market value of Land (in essence collecting a ground rent on behalf of its citizens), the State ensures that all have equal access to Land while itself having a secure source of revenue which is its first requirement.

This is not just a happy coincidence. It follows from Bastiat's statement that it is the State's duty to maintain justice among men, and, as long as there is competition among men for Land, any State which fails to collect the Land rent has failed to perform that duty. Those Libertarians who so strongly espouse individual rights must not neglect the right of every individual to Land, and this right is precisely equal in strength to the right to property in the products of Labour.

The removal of taxes from Labour (income) and from the product of Labour (Capital) will have an extraordinarily positive effect on incentives to work and to produce wealth. Each individual will receive 100% of their pay packet. This will both simplify and clarify the employer/employee contract, meaning that both sides can assess the bargain faster and with greater accuracy. Taking on an extra employee becomes easier and faster. The whole of business accounting is similarly simplified and clarified by the removal of taxation from work and production. The Single Tax on Land value, by ensuring each and every property parcel is put to best use, will push natural resources into the hands of those who will best use them. So Labour (this includes all human endeavour) will be both incentivised to work *and* have the resources on which to work placed in its hands.

That extra wealth will be created in a Single Tax regimen is certain, but how much extra is really speculative. My guess is that it will be anywhere from 50% upward depending on the starting point of the particular economy. The freest and most dynamic States might see the least added advantage while the most repressed would see the most dramatic improvements. It is interesting to note that we have reached our revenue proposition from the argument of individual rights and not from a perspective of maximising wealth creation, yet that is precisely the effect of the proposal. Maximising individual rights will maximise individual wealth and the wealth of society. Now that is a co-incidence! At least at the superficial level.

The natural resource rent

We have followed the natural Law of Property and have arrived at the position espoused by Henry George (1839-1897) that the Land Value Tax or rent is the only legitimate source of revenue for the State. Henry George's name has become synonymous with this method of raising government revenue because of his dedication to the cause. The story of George's life is an interesting one in itself; his pugnacious character, his compassion, his self-education, his literary and oratorical skills, his personal success with the cause and his heroic death in the middle of a political campaign. These, as well as the emotion of taxation and Land ownership in themselves, all contribute to the love-him or hate-him emotion that his name summons.

George was born in Philadelphia, Pennsylvania, U.S.A. in September 1839. He settled in California in 1858 and then New York in 1880; he died in the middle of his campaign for mayor of New York City in October 1897. It is important to note that George came to his conclusion about the 'Single Tax' (as it was frequently called) through direct observation of what happened to Land in western America as it was first settled. He lived through the period when Land was freely available to any settler who would work it, and he saw the consequences of the enclosure of Land by railway and cattle barons – the stuff of many a Western movie.

Having come to these insights, George – sometime typesetter and journalist – proceeded to educate himself in Classical Economics, the dominant economic theory of his day. And from this position he went on to write his best-selling book *Progress and Poverty* (1879), a book which has outsold Adam Smith's *The Wealth of Nations* and Karl Marx's *Das Kapital – put together.*

Classical Economics takes its approach from Adam Smith's *Inquiry into the Nature and Causes of the Wealth of Nations,* that is, it looks at the economy as a whole: how Land, Labour and Capital

Henry George, author of *Progress and Poverty* and advocate of the Single Tax, U.S.A., 1839-1897.

combine to produce wealth, how that wealth is distributed, and how government policy and taxation impact on economic activity. But this approach has its limitations, particularly it was unable to provide a coherent explanation of 'value'.

It fell to the so-called 'Austrian School' of economics to demonstrate that value is subjective, but that it may be objectified at particular points in space and time in the market process. George missed this insight and instead adhered to the now discredited 'Labour Theory' of value; and this lead him into a couple of errors. Firstly he assumed that 'economic rent' (the amount any plot of Land can yield over the marginal plot) is a creature of real life, rather than the useful *theoretical* tool that it was, and is. Then he assumed the price of Land to be no more than this economic rent capitalised.

As a result, George's advocacy of a Single Tax on Land values is open to two interpretations. One school of thought says that the State must collect all the 'economic rent' of Land, replacing as many of the present taxes as this will allow. The other school says that the State must abolish all existing taxes, and instead raise all revenue necessary for government by a Single Tax on Land values.

The important difference between these is that the former school makes the quantity of revenue available to government dependent on the size of the 'economic rent', whether this is more, equal to, or less than the needs of the State. While the latter school argues that it is the needs of the State (predetermined by its functions derived from first principles) which should determine the quantity of revenue to be raised. Both schools agree that once enforced as a tax it will quickly be seen in its true light as a ground rent.

My own view is that the needs of the State can be determined independently of the Georgist argument, but this determination can be made from exactly the same premises we used to arrive at the Georgist conclusion in the first place, namely the natural rights of the individual. *The natural right of individuals to Land (as well as their own Labour) is exactly equal to the natural right of individuals to self-defence*; the first demands the Single Tax on Land value, the second limits State action to defence, police and justice – the Minimal State. Both rights are natural and of equal importance; the Single Tax and the Minimal State belong together. George and Bastiat cannot be separated.

The use of the term 'economic rent' – which rather went out of fashion with George – left him open to accusations of wanting to nationalise Land and of being a socialist, this in spite of his insistence in *Progress and Poverty*, Book viii, Chapter 2 that:

> I do not propose either to purchase or to confiscate private property in land
> ... we may put the proposition into practical form by proposing – *To abolish all taxation save that upon land values.* [Emphasis in the original.]

George's other writings such as *Protection or Free Trade*, show that he was no socialist, indeed the following extract from *A Perplexed Philosopher*, written in 1892 (thirteen years after *Progress and Poverty*, and only five years before he died) shows conclusively that he was averse to a powerful State:

> For in nothing I have ever written or spoken is there any justification for such a characterisation. I am not even a land nationalisationist, as the English and German and Australian land nationalisationists well know. I have never advocated the taking of land by the state or the holding of land

by the state, further than needed for public use; still less the working of land by the state. From my first work on the subject I have advocated what has come to be widely known as 'the single tax'; i.e. the raising of public revenues by taxation on the value of land irrespective of the improvements on it – taxation which, as fast as possible and as far as practicable, should be made to absorb *economic rent* and take the place of all other taxes. And among the reasons I have always urged for this has been the simplification of government and the doing away of the injustice of which governments are guilty in taking from individuals property that rightfully belongs to the individual. I have not gone so far as Mr. Spencer in limiting the functions of government, for I believe that whatever becomes a necessary monopoly becomes a function of the state; and that the sphere of government begins where the freedom of competition ends, since in no other way can equal liberty be assured. But within this line I have always opposed governmental interference. I have been an active, consistent and absolute free trader, and an opponent of all schemes that would limit the freedom of the individual. I have been a stauncher denier of the assumption of the right of society to the possessions of each member, and a clearer and more resolute upholder of the rights of property than has Mr. Spencer. I have opposed every proposition to help the poor at the expense of the rich. I have always insisted that no man should be taxed because of his wealth, and that no matter how many millions a man might rightfully get, society should leave to him every penny of them.

> From *A Perplexed Philosopher* by Henry George, 1937 edition published
> by the Henry George Foundation, Part II, Chapter 2, pages 66-7.
> (My emphasis added.)

George's mistake concerning value and price can be forgiven him, his contribution to the science of economics will, I believe, place him as one of the greatest in this field – along with Bastiat – when the final historical analysis of the subject is written. Indeed powerful movies will yet be made of his life and work, and history will likely show *Progress and Poverty* to have been the climax of Classical Economics. Unfortunately, the suggestion that Land price was determined by the capitalisation of the 'rent' alone, and that Land price would drop to zero under his scheme, has held his name up for ridicule (and scared off many who would have nothing to fear from his proposals). This has obscured the central truth of George as well as the once famous man himself. I suggest that the capitalisation of rent is part of the price of Land, that part which is speculative froth and is blown into bubbles periodically, and which will disappear under this reform. Land will continue to have a price because no two people can own the same plot in the same way as no two people can own a particular Rembrandt, Picasso or the Mona Lisa. There is only one of each and so the price is completely subjective.

The emotional charge surrounding the topics of taxation and Land – as well as George himself – have shrouded the fact that many other men have arrived at the same conclusion independently, both before and after him. Indeed when Henry George travelled on a world speaking tour (March 1890) to New Zealand, he found that the first Land Value Tax in the world had been operating in New Plymouth since 1855. Indeed the idea of a Land tax has been subscribed to by many, including the following: Dr. Thomas Nulty, Bishop of Meath; Adam Smith; John Stuart Mill; The Physiocrats; Thomas Jefferson; Abraham Lincoln; Thomas Paine; Michael Davitt; Winston Churchill; Albert Einstein; Leo Tolstoy; Sun Yat Sen; Milton Friedman and Casper Weinberger (see Appendix C for references). Glowing tributes to George have come from many eminent sources, but perhaps the most pertinent of these has come from the pen of Count Leo Tolstoy:

> They do not argue with Henry George's teaching, they simply do not know it. (There is no other way of dealing with it, for a man who becomes acquainted with it cannot help agreeing with it.)
>
> From *A Great Iniquity*

The argument for the removal of all other taxes does not rest solely on the above mentioned fact that they amount to theft. An equally per-suasive case can be constructed on the implications for incentives: the taxation of Labour and the products of Labour, at any level, discourages the productive process. Removal of these taxes will do much to alleviate the problems of production/distribution that produces poverty. As mentioned in Chapter 3 on natural Law, the State consistently and logically uses the disincentive effects of fines to discourage unwanted behaviour, but ignores these same effects and logic where taxation is concerned (except when taxing alcohol and tobacco on the grounds of discouraging consumption, thereby reducing production as well). Land Value Taxation, on the other hand, would have the beneficial effect of discouraging the holding of Land out of use or under-used. In other words its incentive effects are *positive*. It is the only tax with truly positive effects, and for this reason does not really qualify for the term tax, for it is in fact a rent.

'*To abolish all taxation save that upon land value*' is the proposal; this means phasing out all present general taxes, which would undoubtedly be popular and simple to execute. The introduction of the Land Value Tax, however, despite having been in operation since 1855, is seen by many as problematic because they have difficulty in separating the value of the Land from the value of the improvements made on it. While it is physically impossible to separate the improvements from the Land, professional assessors have no difficulty in separating their values in jurisdictions where an element of Land Value Tax is levied. Overcoming this mental block is the only genuine problem to be encountered. Fortunately it is only a psychological one and not a fundamental or philosophical one, but its resolution is the key to understanding and gaining political support for the proposal. In fact a large body of empirical evidence for its practicability has now been accumulated through the partial implementation of the tax in many areas of the world including New Zealand, Australia, Taiwan, Denmark, Jamaica, and some cities in South Africa and the U.S.A.

Horsman's homeostatic principle

Allied to this body of experience, the following description of a homeo-static principle which would come into effect on the implementation of the Land Value Tax in a market economy, will, I believe, allay any fears that the tax is not practical. Where the system is being set up from scratch, implementation requires that the sale value of each holding of Land be carefully assessed. This may be achieved by taking the sale value of the complete real estate – read from the market – and subtracting from it, an estimated value for all developments and improvements it includes.

Operated by professional assessors using standard codes of practice – including procedures to appeal – and compiled onto Land value maps which the public can inspect, this method will soon produce consistent valuations. Initially these can only be approximation, but to begin with the 'tax' rate will be low so the effect of any inaccuracies will be small. Land value maps would show value contours, ranging from zero/very low for wilderness and marginal Lands, rising to peaks in urban centres or where there are mineral deposits. These maps will rule out inaccuracies among neighbouring or similar holdings.

If then the tax is initiated at a low level on these first approximations, these marginal errors will lead to corresponding overcharging or undercharging on the affected Land types. The market will respond by re-adjusting the price of affected real estate, so that at subsequent re-assessment the errors would be redressed, i.e. the price of real estate with under-charged Land will rise (relatively), and that with over-charged Land will fall (relatively). Subsequent re-assessment will reflect these new market values and the new charges based on them will be more fairly distributed.

This constitutes an inherent feedback mechanism, ensuring that the approximations correspond more and more closely to true valuations at each reassessment. So potent is this feedback mechanism that once set into operation, and all general taxation abolished, *it would be the free market that determined the **tax distribution** and no one else.* Thus the Land Value Tax would be, in reality, a fair market rent (This is why we can say that it is not really a tax.)

All of this is dependent on a free market and on regular and frequent re-assessments, at least annually. The age of computers and electronic communication make this much easier; indeed, given modern advances such as cloud computing, this re-assessment could take place in real time, changing as each new real estate transaction is entered; thus the valuations would be constantly up to date.

Another point to consider is that Land values are much easier to assess than whole properties. The relative simplicity of Land value assessment compared with whole property assessments was underlined in the early 1970s when New South Wales changed from Rates to a Land Value Tax. The Valuer General was able, for the first time ever, to update his entire roll. In America, a leading Land assessor, Ted Gwartney, estimated the cost of whole property re-assessment to be $15-25 per parcel, while a Land only re-assessment would cost only $2-4 per parcel (*Incentive Taxation*, December 1988).

Quite apart from the experience to date of the operation of Land Value Taxation, and apart from the homeostatic mechanism outlined above, the fact that this tax could *partially and accidentally* be levied on the value of improvements is no reason not to implement it. Modern taxation is *consistently and deliberately* levied on such improvements. The aim of this proposal is to get as far away as possible from those taxes: that we might not complete the journey in one move is no reason not to begin it.

Sufficiency of revenue

There is a debate about how much revenue the Land tax may raise; this debate has gone on for years and appears to remain unresolved. Some argue that it will raise only a portion of what is now raised for government, while others argue that it will raise all or almost all that is currently raised by the myriad of taxes levied at present. Others suggest that there may be so much revenue that the State will be able to give every citizen a wage or dividend! Much of the debate seems to centre on what 'rent' actually is; many Georgists appear to hold that the rent of Land is not just the analytical tool or theoretical concept of Classical Economics, but an objective reality that can be taxed at 100%. I believe that the concept of 'rent' of Land is the most valuable contribution of Classical Economics but it is just that: a concept. In the real world this rent is so entangled in the financial returns to property and general taxation – all taxation must be at the expense of this rent anyway – that it is impossible to quantify it with any precision. Rent will only ever become a concrete, objective reality *after* all taxation is abolished and the natural resource rent is the only fund for government.

My view is that the 'Single Tax' will collect whatever amount the government requires at the time. So during wartime when extra revenue is required, the rate can simply be increased to increase the revenue, while during times of peace, the rate can be decreased. In either case, the amount of revenue changes to match the requirement of government without, in any way, affecting the justice involved. It will simply be that during war the returns to Labour and Capital (wages and interest) will decrease, and during peacetime they will increase. The inherent justice of the revenue source will remain constant in both cases.

If this is the case and the revenue volume does not affect its inherent justice, then this is a further compelling reason why the 'Minimal State' has to be paired with the 'Single Tax'. A revenue source that can simply be dialled up or down would place so much temptation on those who hold power that the very concept of power must be challenged; and this can only be successfully done with the Minimal State. This we will address in the following chapter.

If the Land tax were to be substituted penny for penny for all other taxes today it would simply be that some people will pay more while others less. Those 'owners' working or using to the full the resources they own will pay less, while those underutilising the Land will pay more. In fact, only those who hold title deeds will *physically* pay the tax; the little studied or understood phenomenon of 'tax shifting' will ensure that all will contribute their *due* portion. Since it is literally impossible to live or work without using Land, Land 'owners' will see to it that the *due* portion of the tax is passed on to the users in proportion to the use that each make of it. There is no broader base (literally and metaphorically) from which revenue can be raised. Everyone will contribute their due proportion; none can avoid it. And finally, the profession of Land speculation will disappear, at last.

The price of Land paradox

The view that 'rent' is a fixed, set amount rather than the flexible fund I have outlined above has led some to suggest that its collection by government would drive the price of Land to zero (even Henry George alluded to this), arguing that the Land price is no more than the capitalisation of the privately available rent stream. These argue that if Land continues to have a price after Henry George's 'To-abolish-all-taxation-save-that-upon-Land-values' objective is reached then further action is necessary to ensure Land prices become zero. Indeed there is a certain paradox if the free gift of nature – the natural resources – Land, should have a price, after all we premise the whole move away from taxation of Labour and Capital by saying that all should have equal access to Land. To this I can only say, let's see when we get there. The abolition of all taxes upon the active components of the economy, Labour and Capital, will, I believe, be a transformation akin to the abolition of slavery. Let us unite to achieve this monumental task first. Paradoxes generally evaporate in the light of future empirical observations; possibly Land price will turn out to be nothing more than a refundable deposit ensuring that only the sincere will become 'owners'.

The 'ability to pay' principle

One question often asked of the Land Value Tax is whether it accords with the *'ability to pay'* principle. Now this principle (or *'maxim'* of taxation as Adam Smith called it) was only the first of four which he set out in his famous work *The Wealth of Nations*, published in 1776. It seems a little peculiar that this should be the only maxim out of the four that is regularly recited; perhaps this has more than a little to do with the fact that it chimes with one of the catchwords of Marxist doctrine, *'From each according to his ability ...'*. Smith's second maxim was that tax liability should be 'certain': on this a Land Value Tax scores very highly, while income (ability to pay) taxes score very poorly. We should note that Smith rated this certainty principle well ahead of the ability principle in the following words.

> The certainty of what each individual ought to pay is, in taxation, a matter of so great importance that a very considerable degree of inequality ... is not so great an evil as a very small degree of uncertainty.
>
> *Op. cit.*, Book 5, Chapter 2, Part 2

Smith's third maxim, that the time of payment should be convenient for the payee, has become largely outdated but we can note that a Land Value Tax may be billed monthly or at any other interval suitable for the citizen.

On Smith's final maxim, that the tax should be efficient to collect, the Land Value Tax tops the list of all taxes due to its certainty, its ease of administration and the impossibility of hiding Land; while the 'ability to pay' or income taxes score very poorly here again.

Finally, Adam Smith explicitly denounces taxes on the wages of Labour, describing them as *'Absurd and destructive...'* (*Op. cit.*, Book 5, Chapter 2, Part 2, Article III.)

In conclusion, we see that the 'ability to pay' maxim is not the only, or even the most important maxim that its author wished to make known, and it *cannot be the final arbiter of a just tax*. Furthermore, since we have derived the Land Value Tax from a principle of high order – namely justice in property rights – it is illogical to disallow or even question it on a principle (maxim) of lower order.

That said, the Land tax can be considered as related to ability to pay, because the tax base (Land value) is directly related to what willing buyers are prepared to pay for Land they wish to occupy. In that sense individuals determine their tax liability according to what they can afford. But if the owner is not able to afford the tax on a site, because its value has gone up, he is at least in the comfortable position of being able to rent it out to someone who can put it to good use. Or he may sell it at a profit since Land values rise continuously in the long term.

If, in spite of all the above, the case of the little old widow who is no longer able to afford to live in her home of long-standing – because the district has become a valuable commercial area – is brought up, there are several points to bear in mind in this situation.

1   Since the property has become so valuable, the widow has the possibility of paying on the strength of a mortgage, which would finally be settled by her estate.
2   We must remember that our proposal includes the abolition of all other taxes which over a lifetime allows for a greater nest-egg accumulation. So this problem will disappear over time.
3   If the widow sells out, or sells half her garden for an office block development we should note that she does so from a choice of least bad options; and we should compare that situation with the many who are moved – without choice – in road building or other State schemes.
4   Finally, if the defendant for the widow is still not satisfied, he should consider the rights of all the potential employees of the business being held up by the widow: all the potential production and employment lost – and lives thereby made less. Is the move of one person such a big thing, particularly if she comes away with a substantial cheque in her pocket? Capital-gains-tax-free to boot!

Some economic and ecological observations

The benefits and implications of the Single Tax form a vast subject in themselves and I do not intend to rehearse them all here, but because revenue is of paramount importance to the State and hugely influential in all our lives, a few selected topics will be addressed. There are a number of Georgist organisations around the world where these debates are fully explored; see Resources at the end of this book.

To begin, we may make a general statement at the level of human experience. Since this reform goes a long way to restore justice in property rights we can expect that much of the resentment and other hurt feelings engendered by the present injustices will disappear, and greater harmony among people is more likely.

Practically speaking, there will be a fully functioning economy, the like of which has rarely been experienced in human history:

1 *Full* Labour employment,
2 *Optimal* Capital employment, and
3 *Appropriate* natural resource usage.

Putting figures on it

It is often asked how this proposal will affect different classes of taxpayers, individuals, families, industries, etc. as the media like to portray at budget times. This method of economic analysis is facile in the extreme and ultimately very misleading. There are four main reasons why this analytic process is too childish to be used for such a serious issue, in fact these reasons also hold for standard taxes so beware of being misled by such analyses.

1 Due to the phenomenon of 'tax shifting', knowledge of who actually *pays* each tax is very limited, thus it is very difficult to forecast who will benefit from the abolished taxes, and to what extent. To illustrate: Value Added Tax is levied on producers, but is actually 'shifted' onto consumers through higher prices; income taxes are levied on individuals but – it can be argued – are largely 'shifted' onto business. There is no consensus amongst economists on the phenomenon of tax shifting, so the only thing we can say for certain is that the private sector as a whole will benefit as the burden of taxation is lifted off enterprise. There is, however, one point on which economists generally agree, and it is one of the few points of consensus in this profession: a Land Value Tax cannot be shifted unduly.
2 The abolition of existing taxes will increase opportunities and incentives to work, leading to full employment and rising incomes. This extra income and production cannot be computed in advance with certainty, but we can be certain about its direction.
3 Government involvement in the productive processes of the economy will disappear, leaving a much reduced need for government revenue. This will leave a similarly increased amount of money in individual's hands.
4 The most serious objection, however, to any attempt to 'put figures on it' stems from the fact that the free market will be the sole determinant of the Land tax as discussed earlier in this chapter. It is *de facto* impossible to say how the free market will distribute the

charge. Furthermore, *the proposed reform is likely to change fundamentally the whole pattern of economic and social relationships, so that any interpolation from the present pattern is likely to be wide of the mark.* It is therefore not only virtually impossible to put figures on it, but attempting to do so is inevitably misleading, as are current budget time illustrations.

The Single Tax and the environment

The environmental movement has grown considerably since World War II, from a few idealists to today's consensus of governments globally. The sense of impending catastrophic change in the climate is being used by those who want the State to have even more power over individual lives. The concept of Global Governance is even being touted as a remedy for the problems of the climate and the environment. Some in the free world are even holding up China's 'one child' policy as the answer to the problem.

The problem with most of the political solutions is that they end up merely transferring the problem elsewhere or even causing more problems. State action requires more taxation which in turn further affects economic margins and thus the environment. So if attempting to lift oneself by the bootlaces causes a pain in the back, the solution is to let go and not to pull harder! Otherwise the pain will only get worse.

I arrived at the Single Tax solution directly as a result of an enquiry into the root cause of man's environmental destructiveness, and only later discovered Henry George. The chain of reasoning is as follows. The bulk of tax revenue for the majority of the world's major economies comes from income related taxes and, till recently, this has fallen more and more onto lower incomes. This is little more than taxation of Labour, and it has had the effect of marginalising much human scale work which must then be performed by some technology or it is no longer performed at all. Historically, the increase in taxes on bread and butter wages bears a high degree of coincidence with the increase of pollution; and of course increased unemployment is the other side of the coin.

The effect of abolishing all taxes on income would be to remove this premium on Labour – and thus on time – and bring about a far greater concern for the details which go to make up our environment, as well as removing a great disincentive to employment. Human scale work is normally the most environmentally benign way of performing any function; thus to tax work is to ask for environmental trouble. This holds for both the man-made environment as well as the natural. A little thought will reveal that taxing the produce of Labour – goods and services – is only one step from taxing work (although it does equally tax techno-logical production). Therefore the only way for government to raise revenue without taxing work or people is to tax Land values.

More philosophically, the restoration of the rights of all in the planet (achieved by the Single Tax solution) will surely mean that it will be cared for – after all no one *wants* to live in a soiled nest. And *the Single Tax proposal will do far more to harmonise man's relation with nature than all the legislation ever produced could hope to do.* These benefits would far outweigh the effects that the Land tax would have in bringing some presently unspoilt natural resources into use. By ensuring that settlement patterns form contiguous units rather than 'Swiss cheese', much of the currently threatened areas would become unthreatened again. The point is that without taxation, *work and development will naturally tend to be ecologically harmonious.*

> Without taxation, work and development will naturally tend to be ecologically harmonious.

We might even speculate that the taxation of Labour has been a conscious or unconscious effort by those who stand to gain from the exploitation of fossil fuels, to increase their consumption, since fossil fuels ultimately tend to substitute for human work. The removal of taxes from work and production will tend to reduce fossil fuel dependency, an aim considered worthy by most people.

*

The connection between the commute to work and back each day with the Single Tax may not appear obvious, while its connection with air pollution should be crystal clear. If commute distances could be halved or quartered it would improve environmental quality immensely.

So how could the Single Tax dramatically reduce commuting? It is all to do with the cost of relocating. Whether it is the business moving to where people live, or people moving to where the jobs are, or a bit of both, the point is the same. At present there are very high costs associated with selling one's home (or business premises) and buying another. These costs may be Stamp Duties, Value Added Tax, Capital Gains Tax or other, and they all majorly disincentivize property transfers, and they would all disappear under a Single Tax regimen. In fact they would have to be the first to be abolished since it is important for the working of the valuation system that there is a good, fluid property market from which to assess values.

The Single Tax removes enormous financial hurdles from jobs and people moving closer together so we can expect them to do just that, reducing the insanity of gridlocked traffic and road chaos.

There is a further point to consider. During times of Land value booms, as was the case for the decade up to 2007, people actually tend to move further away from work trading up their small homes in high value, work rich areas to larger homes in lower value dormitory towns. The Single Tax would remove this pressure as well, by removing the speculative froth from Land prices. With more local work, villages and small towns would become more viable and so Land prices would be more even over the whole territory of the State. Work and communities would form organic wholes rather than disparate entities; this would have the added benefit of a more wholesome social mix.

*

In this chapter we have examined the means whereby the State may fund itself in a manner that is completely and inherently just. With the exception of fines and penalties that the Judicial system may impose,[8] this is the only means the State can have to raise revenue. All other schemes that have existed or still exist are immoral and oppressive robbery, no matter how long they have existed or how great the argument in defence of them. 100% security of private property in the products of Labour, as well as the rights of every individual to the planet's resources, trumps them all. Natural Law dictates the Land Value Tax.

Proponents of the Land Value Tax have observed the providential fact that the value of Land increases with the increase in population and improvement in the economy, making sure that there will always be ample funding for the State. This seems too coincidental to be a matter of chance and seems to be more like a product of design. Not so much an invisible hand but an invisible, wise and generous Mind.

---

[8] Duties may be placed on the likes of Carbon Dioxide emissions, raising revenue at the same time as deterring or altering the economic margin of the use of materials and processes that produce such emissions. But these are impositions of Justice ministry and not Finance.

This gives rise to a curious feeling that when we ask the right questions we find that nature is no longer a wilderness that produces weeds and thorns, but a beautiful garden in which one day we will be able to live and walk with our God.

CHAPTER 5

The Minimal State

*'Ask immensely simple questions ... when the answers are
simple too, then you hear God thinking.'*
Jacob Bronowski

*'The chief foundations of all States... are
good laws and good arms...'*
Nicolo Machiavelli

T HE MINIMAL STATE presents no opportunity for vainglory. The
power and right of all citizens to defend themselves is vested in the
State and becomes the State's sole function. There is no room for
the pseudo-generosity of Ministers and politicians to hand-out free
education, free health services, free welfare or jobs or factories or homes
or anything else.

The Minimal State's glory is that it presents individuals – and voluntary
associations of individuals – with the greatest possible opportunity to
do whatever good seems right to them. By ensuring justice among its
citizens, the Minimal State does away with the antagonisms and resent-
ments common to subjects of modern States, and which sap the strength
and power from those who would like to help others. Whether it be
caring for the less fortunate and the sick, or educating the ignorant,
helping out those caught up in wars and conflicts or those struck by
natural disasters, or protecting wildlife or ecosystems, or simply plying
a trade. Even the largest projects that man can conceive such as the
exploration of Mars and the furthest realms of the universe may be carried
out by those with the vision and drive, and they will be unhindered by

the bureaucratic nature of all government. Money will be readily available for such projects when the massive crusher of taxation has been destroyed.

The concept of the Minimal State is not an ancient one and is as yet little known or understood. The closest we find in ancient cultures is in the Greece that gave democracy to the world. At that time, the idea that all people were *equal under the law* was at least as important as democracy and was given a special name 'isonomia' which has been anglicised as 'isonomy'. Weather forecasters use the related term 'isobar' to link areas of equal atmospheric pressure. To Herodotus, isonomy was *'the most beautiful of all names of a political order.'*[9]

The Minimal State is identical to the Night Watchman State of the Classical Liberal tradition, but is based on entirely different theoretical foundations. The Night Watchman is the image used to portray a State that keeps a watchful eye open for intruders but will not otherwise take any intervening actions, and so it is just like the Minimal State. The difference is that Classical Liberalism comes to this ideal State from examining the real and/or theoretical consequences of a State which gets involved in anything other than defence, police and justice; the unwritten assumption being that the State potentially could go beyond this, and of course in practice it did. The Minimal State, on the other hand, comes from the argument that all State powers derive from the individual and thus *cannot* be extended beyond this minimum under any circumstances. Thus the title of Father of the Minimal State must go to Frederic Bastiat, who not only saw this truth but gave his all to promulgate and promote it in the France of the 1840s. Since that time, Bastiat has been virtually forgotten in his own Land, and – as the dark cloud of communism spread its monstrous State over the minds of the world – the Minimal State concept almost died again. But in recent years a revival of interest has taken place and a new star rises in the intellectual firmament.

The concept rose to new heights with the publication of Robert Nozick's blockbuster *Anarchy, State and Utopia* (1974),[10] which won a National Book Award as well as the praise of friend and foe alike. Further scholarship arrived in 1987 when Norman Barry published his book, *On Classical Liberalism and Libertarianism*, which dissects the main schools of these

---

[9] Herodotus, *Histories*, iii. 80.

[10] Published by Basic Books Inc.

various traditions. There are a number of interesting parallels between these two men. Both were university professors, Nozick at Harvard (Professor of Philosophy), Barry at Buckingham (Professor of Social and Political Theory); both were modern giants in this field, both publishing books essential to this author's work, and both, sadly, died relatively young: Robert Nozick 1938-2002; Norman P. Barry 1944-2008. I met Barry but not Nozick. (See Appendix B for their photos.)

Nozick

In *Anarchy, State and Utopia*, Nozick sets himself to counter anarchist arguments against the Minimal State. He begins by assuming a world of morally imperfect people in a state of 'Statelessness'. Then, by a process of voluntary association, he constructs commercial 'protective agencies' which perform judicial services for their members and defends them against aggression. Assuming these protective associations are always morally perfect, Nozick argues that competition between them will lead to one 'dominant protective agency' in each territorial area. This, he concludes, is a Minimal State; hence he argues the legitimacy of the Minimal State against its anarchic detractors.

If Nozick had allowed the moral imperfections of the people to inhabit their associations, he would have concluded that, sooner or later, one of the protective agencies would become morally corrupt and use its monopoly of force to further itself at the expense of other associations, as well as its own members, becoming a mimic of modern States. He would have arrived at the Conflict Theory of the origin of the State. Sadly, he not only fails to be consistent in his logic and reach this conclusion, but he expressly denies the validity of the Franz Oppenheimer (Conflict) thesis, referring to it as *'an illegitimate route to the State'*. Nozick fails to acknowledge that his construction is a theoretical tool while Oppenheimer is describing historical reality. This confusion of reality and theory, and his inconsistent logic mar an otherwise sublime work. Nozick's greatest effect has been to give validity to the discussion of the Minimal State among intellectuals.

Barry

Professor Barry's book *On Classical Liberalism and Libertarianism* is a more straightforward survey of the philosophical foundations of freedom, rich in information and insight. But Barry too fails to see the importance of the Oppenheimer thesis. In Chapter 9 he says:

… Oppenheimer's analysis is deficient in that it concentrates almost entirely on external aggression by one social grouping against another as the cause of the rise of States to the exclusion of internal processes within communities.

The point Barry misses here is that it is precisely the *monopoly* of force involved in the aggression that is *the defining feature* of the State. Whether any particular State in history arose by the agreement of its inhabitants, or could have done, is not the question (the United States of America and Switzerland among others may have arisen in this way). The foundation of the State as *an historical entity* is entirely based on conquest and bloodshed. Even the U.S.A. was not without its baptism in the blood of the native peoples, and it has subsequently acquired all the trappings of the aggressive State of Oppenheimer.

The importance of Barry's consummate work is his conclusion that Classical Liberalism cannot provide the philosophical foundations for freedom; only Political Libertarianism with its basis in individual rights is fit for the task; and of all the various Libertarian schools, only that of Richard Nozick comes near to producing a complete underpinning for fully fledged freedom.

The opinion of both these scholars in respect to Franz Oppenheimer may be the key to unlocking their common blind spot. One of Oppenheimer's most trenchant conclusions was the common heritage of all people in the Land, and to effect this George's Single Tax was the answer. We find Nozick's dismissal of George in *Anarchy, State and Utopia*, Chapter 7, is total and completely unsubstantiated. Barry, on the other hand, consistently uses Georgist type questions concerning the validity of title to Land, and he would appear to be open to the Land Value Tax:

> The question of legitimacy in landownership is likely to become crucially important in the future development of libertarian thought.
>
> *Op. Cit.*, Chapter 8, Section Vi

In the past, the Minimal State has itself been considered unjust because the only means its adherents could conceive of funding government was to levy taxes on its citizens. Thus, because taxation, as it has been practiced throughout history, was inevitably unjust and oppressive, so the Minimal State has been considered in the same light. This logic has led many Libertarians and deep thinkers to drop the Minimal State and pursue some anarchistic theory or other.

We can now see that the Minimal State, by raising its revenue from Land values, can avoid this pitfall and once more appeal to those who desire that the State pursue only the defence of justice. The majority of Georgists are not Minimal Staters, and the majority of Minimal Staters are not Georgists. It is my hope that each will share the vision of the other and present to the world the gift it has so long needed. Actually these are the two sides of one coin.

Let us now examine in detail the Minimal State that we have arrived at. From the last chapter, we can see that the Land Value Tax may be used to raise whatever revenue may be required by the State. Whether the tax is small or large, it is equally just. So long as the tax extracts more from higher value sites and less from lower value ones, it will ensure equality of access for all people. So long as the relative differentials remain between sites of different value, it does not matter what the *volume* of the tax take is. The fact is that the Minimal State will require far less revenue at its greatest need than any modern State requires.

Now that we are assured of both the justice and sufficiency of the revenue source for the Minimal State, we may now discuss its merits *per se*. Bastiat and Oppenheimer have demonstrated that force is essential to the continuance of the State. Indeed it is the *sine qua non* for the State's existence. So long as there exist threats to its citizens from both inside and outside its domain, the State's force will be required and this is its sole function. This force cannot logically be used to perform any function other than the negation of injustice. In this way the natural right that any individual possesses to self-defence may be elevated into an organised system, increasing efficiency and fitness to an extraordinary degree. This is both the Minimal State and the maximum legitimate State.

This Minimal State will undoubtedly be hard for many to accept, brought up in a world where power is generally removed from individuals (through oppressive taxation) and handed over to the State, to perform by proxy, for us. Debilitating as this experience has been and still is, there is constant pressure from society (as opposed to lobby groups) for freedom from coercion in all its forms. So long as freedom is the watchword of the 'free world', we may be justified in the belief that the Minimal State will one day happen – though maybe not overnight.

The prospect of the future State that defends the freedom of all and nothing else, may be disquieting. So entranced have we become by the modern State and its power, and so unused and unable have we become to making a myriad of individual decisions for ourselves and our loved ones in those areas where the State has assumed responsibility, that the prospect of this power and responsibility reverting to the individual seems awesome.

The State has become our god. We worship[11] it with our votes, our money and our thoughts. We expect it to heal us (with its health service), to lead us into the truth (with its education system), and to love us tenderly from the cradle to the grave (with its social security system). We turn our backs on God's creation of family, friends and community and our relationships with all individuals. We have the State as our lord and saviour; we no longer need each other. The prophecy from Revelation Chapter 13 concerning the beast from the sea is fulfilled, verse 8: '*All the inhabitants of the world will worship it*'. Indeed, the whole world worships the State; this is Stateolatry.

When we say that the Minimal State's function is limited to defence of its citizens and that it should not organise any positive action, this does not mean that those things should not be performed at all – far from it. It only means that there is complete freedom, under the law, for individuals, companies and associations to organise whatever activities they will, and – if the State is limited to its necessary purpose – the freedom to do so will be greater than at any time in human history. Indeed the incentive to perform the activities presently organised by force of law will come from the necessity imposed on individuals by nature. And, because that dead-weight of oppression – the crusher of taxation – will have been removed, the ability of individuals to respond to natural necessity will be immensely increased. This is not so difficult to imagine when it is considered that all the activities organised by any State originally began as private enterprise – including even the State's legitimate functions!

The enormous amount of voluntary effort that is evident today, for a great variety of causes, including political, environmental, social, economic, and religious further demonstrates this and points to the potential. If all this can be accomplished under a system of legally enshrined injustice – which actually causes most of the problems – what

---

[11] Apologies to those who think they have no faith, for raising the topic of worship in the subject of political philosophy. But whether one worships Jesus, Yaweh or Allah; ancestral spirits, football heroes or gurus; cars, jewellery, money or clothes; spouse, job or hobby; science or self – man is designed to worship, naturally worships, and he cannot help himself. Most would not even think that they are in fact worshipping. Many worship more than one god, and the State has become probably the most universal, most subtle, and most pervasive god that man has yet kow-towed to. Many who would consider themselves to be monotheists and who should know better also worship the State.

will the limits of human cooperation be when justice finally reigns and the principal cause of the troubles has been removed?

Bastiat pointed out in *The Law* that unjust laws tend to erase from people's minds the difference between justice and injustice. So if justice becomes enshrined in State law, people will more easily differentiate between right and wrong and therefore treat others justly. But if the State treats its citizens unjustly, then they are more likely to treat each other in the same fashion.

The term 'social justice' has become an emotive catch-phrase, but is really an oxymoron. Society is not a concrete entity that can suffer injustice. It takes real people to suffer injustice and each case must be treated separately if justice is to be done. Only when all individuals in society can be said to have access to all the redress they require may it be said that justice reigns in that society.

The State is without doubt the greatest source of injustice that humans suffer under. Should we continue to allow the State through its laws to deprive many of access to opportunity (Land), and satisfying lifestyles (earned income), driving individuals to seek fulfilment in self-destructive ways (such as taking drugs)? The question of what a private citizen does to himself by abusing drugs, for example, is not a matter for the State. If the individual is not harming others (or in a position to harm, such as driving a vehicle or parenting a child), the State has no jurisdiction. But the State that deprives and oppresses its citizens is *the* single largest cause of social unhappiness, driving individuals to self-destruction. The answer is to remove the oppression and deprivation, and allow everyone equal access to opportunity. What individuals make of those opportunities is up to themselves and not any business of the State.

Herbert Spencer writing in *Social Statics* makes the point that as the State has taken over what should be individual functions, these faculties in individuals have atrophied. The reverse is also true: these faculties would immediately begin to grow as they were again exercised:

> The ultimate result of shielding men from the effects of folly is to fill the world with fools.
> Herbert Spencer, *Essays: Scientific, Political, and Speculative*, Vol. 3, 'State-tamperings with Money and Banks', first published in *The Westminster Review*, January 1858, paragraph 460

It is now time to reverse the process. Individuals must be allowed to be responsible for themselves so they may learn in the school of life how best to behave.

The Minimal State and the Single Tax

We saw in the last chapter that the Single Tax – because it is such an efficient revenue source – would place huge temptations in the hands of those in power that it actually *requires* the Minimal State provisions to ensure that this high octane political fuel cannot be misused. Now we come across a similar link the other way round, where the Minimal State provisions actually demand the Single Tax.

The Minimal State is closely allied to the Night Watchman State of the Classical Liberal tradition, and as such it has come closer to having had a real innings already. The problem with it, in reality then and in theory still, is that restricting State functions to defence and police only without tackling the injustice of Land ownership, condemns most to a condition of slavery or serfdom. The story of Robinson Crusoe and his slave, Man-Friday, makes the point. On a limited plot of Land, it makes no difference if Crusoe owns Friday or the Land. The effect is precisely the same: Crusoe gets all his work done by Friday. Crusoe gets the whole week off – as well as the weekend – every week! Just like our Land speculators. So the State that does not ensure equal access to its natural resources for all its citizens becomes a Welfare State to compensate. But it is poor compensation, and it is much better for individuals to have free reign for their industrious activities and to have complete freedom of choice as to how they spend the resulting income. The defence-and-police-only State demands justice in Land ownership. The Minimal State demands the Single Tax.

So the two game-changing proposals of this book, the Single Tax and the Minimal State – Henry George and Frederick Bastiat – actually cry out for one another.

> The Single Tax without the Minimal State is an invitation to totalitarianism – the exploitation of the masses by the political class; while the Minimal State without the Single Tax is exploitation of the masses by the landed.

They must be joined together to work properly. The Single Tax without the Minimal State is an invitation to totalitarianism, the exploitation of the masses by the political class, while the Minimal State without the Single Tax is exploitation of the masses by the Landed. The implementation of either proposal without the other can only lead to massive exploitation; and so the two must be conjoined.

This is neither a happy coincidence nor a forced conclusion. Both the Single Tax and the Minimal State derive from propositions that place the rights of the individual citizens at the top of the agenda: people matter most! The Single Tax comes from saying that each individual has an equal right to the earth's natural resources and that the fruit of his Labour is totally his, while the Minimal State comes from saying that individual's rights to self-defence are the sole legitimate origin of State power so it must be limited to just that. Both proposals come from rights inherent in the individual, so it should be no surprise that they actually require each other; one without the other is nonsense.

This conclusion holds strong implications for proponents of both stripes. Georgists need to take on board the Libertarian agenda, while Libertarians must include the Georgist Single Tax. Here, perhaps, is the reason why both have struggled for so long but with such limited success. Now, if both get together then, I believe, the world will get the true picture and take both proposals to heart.

*

In Part I we attempted to discover the nature of the State. Having looked at its origins and history we eventually discovered through natural Law that, in essence, *the State can be nothing other than the individual's right of self-defence combined into one common force*. Though we introduced the Minimal State at the end of Part I, we did not begin the first of our three proposals in Part II with it, instead we continued the natural Law discussion to uncover the means of funding such a State. We took this approach because the Minimal State has been proposed by others before, but never has it been combined with the Single Tax. So, in the previous chapter, we not only explored how to raise revenue without taxation, but we went into detail concerning the theory, history, implementation and implications of the idea. In the current chapter we have taken the Minimal State, introduced at the end of Part I, and worked it up to detailed sketch, but it will require much more space to lay out fully; it will take nearly half of this book (all of Part III and much of Part IV) to complete this topic. But before we do that we will present the third of our three proposals, the free Judicial Service.

CHAPTER 6

Justice – Finally!

'But let justice roll down like a river, righteousness
like a never failing stream'
Amos 5:24

T HE MONOPOLY on force, which the Minimal State requires, guaran-
teeing that it will be able to deal with any and all threats, imposes
another limit on the State's behaviour. But this time it is a perimeter it
has not yet reached: *The State must provide its citizens with a judicial service*
that imposes no charges on those who come to it for justice.

The transfer, by individuals, of their naturally held right to use force
for their defence implies that the organisation to which that right is given
(or shared) will use it immediately and
without qualification as soon as any of its
constituent members require it. Just as an
individual without the State would act to
defend himself (his life, liberty and property)

**If justice costs money
then it cannot be
Justice.**

so must the State use its monopoly of force to effect that defence. Thus
it is the duty of the State to provide a judicial *service* which protects all
individuals. If the State asks for payment for doing that which is its duty,
it fails in that duty. If justice costs money, the less well-off will receive less
of it and that is injustice. If justice can be bought, it is not Justice.

A free judicial service is clearly implied in the Minimal State of Nozick.
Though he nowhere states it explicitly, the fee for membership of the
'Protective Agency' entitles the member to the processes of justice
without further charge. Under a 'Dominant Protective Agency' (the
equivalent of the Minimal State), the 'subscriber' (citizen) appears to be

75

entitled to this judicial service free of charge. Sadly Nozick does not spell this out.

The only person who has written about this aspect of State function is Herbert Spencer. In a letter from 1843 (the early Spencer), letter X. of a compilation of letters under the title, 'The Proper Sphere of Government', in *The Man Versus the State*, published by Liberty Classics in 1981, we find the following:

Had our governors always taken care duly to perform their original and all-important functions – had the administration of justice ever stood pre-eminent in their eyes – had it at all times been considered as the one thing needful, and had no other questions ever been entertained at its expense, then might their interference in matters with which they had no concern, have been more excusable. But it is not so. To the long list of their sins of commission, we have to add the sin of omission; and most grievously has the nation suffered from their neglect, as well as from their officiousness.

Describe to an unbiased arbitrator the relationship existing between a people and a government. Tell him that the legislature is a body deputed by the nation to keep order, to protect person and property, and that these are its most important, if not its only duties. Tell him that every man practically gives in his allegiance to this body – that he annually pays towards its support a considerable portion of his earnings – that he sacrifices to it his personal independence – and that he does these things, in the expectation of receiving from it the advantages of that protection, which it is presumed to give in return for such deprivations.

Explain all this, and then ask him to state, in what manner he should expect the government, to fulfil its part of the contract. He would say that when the subjects had paid their taxes, and submitted themselves to the authorities, they had done all that could be required of them – that it remained with those authorities to carry home to every man the benefits of civil order – that the revenue was subscribed by the people for the express purpose of defraying the charges of this protective establishment – and that, after men had thus prepaid the government, it would be a most unjust proceeding for that government to put him to additional expense whenever it was called upon to perform its duty towards them. From these consider-ations he would infer that it behoved the State to establish courts of justice, which should be easy of access, speedy in their decisions, and in which every man should be able to obtain the protection of the law, free of cost. Such is the obviously equitable conclusion at which a conscientious umpire would arrive.

How widely different from the reality! Our legislators tax the people to a most exorbitant extent; squander the money thus wrested from the toiling artisan in the support of institutions for the benefit of the rich; maintain, by its aid, standing armies to ensure popular subjection; and, when the misused subject demands of the government that it defend him in the exercise of his rights and privileges – when he asks it to fulfil the duties for which it was instituted – when he requests it to do for him that for which he has already paid it so extravagantly – what is its conduct? Does it, without further reward, fully and fairly administer the laws? Does it send forth its officers, commanding them diligently

Herbert Spencer, proponent of
the free judicial service,
United Kingdom,
1820-1903.

to secure to every one, that protection which he has sacrificed so much to obtain? Does it take up the cause of the poor man, and defend him against the aggressions of his rich neighbour?

No! it does none of these things. It turns over the complainant to the tender mercies of solicitors, attorneys, barristers, and a whole legion of law officers. It drains his purse with charges for writs, briefs, affidavits, subpoenas, fees of all kinds, and expenses innumerable. It involves him in all the mazy intricacies of common courts, chancery courts, suits, counter-suits, and appeals; and thousands of times has it overwhelmed with irretrievable ruin, the man whose person and property it was bound to defend. And this is our 'glorious constitution'!

We pity the poor subjects of oriental despotism. We view their absolute form of government with contempt. We turn from it to contemplate what we call our 'free institutions' with pride, and congratulate ourselves upon the superiority of our condition. Yet might these autocrat-ridden people hold up to the world's scorn, the results of our seemingly 'free institutions'. Many and many a case could they point out in this 'land of liberty', of misery and famine, inflicted by the rich man's tyranny – of wrongs endured, because money was wanting wherewith to purchase redress – of rights unclaimed, because contention with the powerful usurper was useless – aye, hundreds upon hundreds might they find, whose hollow cheeks and tattered clothing, could bear testimony to the delusiveness of English justice. And then, by way of contrast, they could tell of the active and even-handed legislation of many an absolute monarch. Countless examples might they point out, of justice freely and fairly administered by Eastern sultans – instances where the poor and weak could pour their tales of tyranny into the ear of the monarch himself, and obtain assistance – where wealth and interest were not required to secure protection; neither were they any shield to the oppressor. Fie upon Englishmen that they should continue to praise and venerate a mere shadow – to pride and congratulate themselves upon the possession of what is daily demonstrated to be a hollow mockery! How long will men allow themselves to be cheated by an empty name? Not only has our government done those things which it ought not to have done, but it has left undone those things which it ought to have done; and truly may it be said that there is no health in it.

Let us, therefore, bear in mind that by permitting our rulers to spend their time – and our money – in the management of matters over which they ought to have no control, we not only entail upon ourselves the evils arising from their mischievous legislation, but likewise those resulting from the neglect of their real duties.

Most democratic States have a State prosecution service which acts in so-called 'criminal' actions, distinguishing those from 'civil' actions. This much we may at least be thankful for, but is there here a distinction without a difference? Because someone has not physically stolen another person's goods, but has merely failed to comply with a trade contract (e.g. failed to pay for the goods), does not decriminalise him. Yet here the injured party must, in addition to all his payments to the State (to which he has handed over his powers of redress), pay out further to instigate judicial proceedings, which may or may not prove successful. Thus he risks not only his 'stolen' goods but his legal fees on top of it all. This is not just. *All* wrongs must be amenable to free judicial proceedings – without exception.

This proposal – to have a fully-fledged judicial *service*, funded by the State and costing nothing for the participating protagonists (the guilty party could, of course, be charged with costs for both sides as part of the sentence) – may elicit a strange reaction which Spencer notes in *Social Statics*, Chapter 21, Section 5:

There are not wanting, however, men who defend the present state of things – who actually argue that government should perform but imperfectly what they allow to be its special function. Whilst, on the one hand, they admit, that administration of justice is the vital necessity of civilised life, they maintain, on the other, that justice may be administered too well! 'For,' say they, 'were law cheap, all men would avail themselves of it. Did there exist no difficulty in obtaining justice, justice would be demanded in every case of violated rights. Ten times as many appeals would be made to the authorities as now. Men would rush into legal proceedings on the slightest provocation; and litigation would be so enormously increased as to make the remedy worse than the disease.'

Such is the argument; an argument involving either a gross absurdity or an unwarranted assumption. For observe: when this great multiplication of law proceedings under a gratuitous administration of justice is urged as a reason why things should remain as they are, it is implied that the evils attendant upon the rectification of all wrongs, would be greater than are the evils attendant upon submission to those wrongs. Either the great majority of civil aggressions must be borne in silence as now, or must be adjudicated upon as then; and the allegation is that the first alternative is preferable. But if ten thousand litigations are worse than ten thousand injustices, then one litigation is worse than one injustice. Which means that, as a general principle, any appeal to law for protection is a greater evil than the trespass complained of. Which means that it would be better to have no administration of justice at all!

If for the sake of escaping this absurdity it be assumed that, as things now are, all *great* wrongs are rectified – that the costliness of law prevents insignificant ones only from being brought into court, and that consequently the above inference cannot be drawn – then, either denial is given to the obvious fact that, by the poverty they inflict, many of the greatest wrongs incapacitate their victims from obtaining redress, and to the obvious fact that the civil injuries suffered by the masses, though *absolutely* small, are relatively great; or else it is taken for granted that on nine-tenths of the population, who are too poor to institute legal proceedings, no civil injuries of moment are ever inflicted!

Nor is this all. It is not necessarily true that making the law easy of access would increase litigation. An opposite effect might be produced. The prophecy is vitiated by that very common mistake of calculating the result of some new arrangement on the assumption that all other things would remain as they are. It is taken for granted that under the hypothetical regime just as many transgressions would occur as at present. Whereas any candid observer can see that most of the civil offences now committed, are committed in *consequence* of the inefficiency of our judicial system;

'For sparing justice feeds iniquity.'

It is the difficulty that he knows there will be in convicting him, which tempts the knave to behave knavishly. Were not the law so expensive and so uncertain, dishonest traders would never risk the many violations of it they now do. The trespasses of the wealthy against the poor would be rare, were it not that the aggrieved have practically no remedy. Mark how, to the man who contemplates wronging his fellow, our legal system holds out promises of impunity. Should his proposed victim be one of small means, there is the likelihood that he will not be able to carry on a lawsuit: here is encouragement. Should he possess enough money, why, even then, having, like most people, a great dread of litigation, he will probably bear his loss unresistingly: here is further encouragement. Lastly, our plotter remembers that, should his victim venture an action, judicial decisions are very much matters of accident, and that the guilty are often rescued by clever counsel: here is still more encouragement. And so, all things considered, he determines to chance it. Now, he would never decide thus were legal protection efficient. Were the administration of law prompt, gratuitous, and certain, those probabilities and possibilities which now beckon him on to fraudulent acts would vanish.

Civil injuries wittingly committed would almost cease. Only in cases where both parties sincerely believed themselves right, would judicial arbitration be called for; and the number of such cases is comparatively small. Litigation, therefore, so far from *increasing* on justice being made easy of obtainment, would probably *decrease*.

Herbert Spencer's logic is impeccable and still holds. A free judicial service would probably lead to a decrease in both the volume of litigation as well as the number of offences being committed. These prospects by themselves are surely a sufficient commendation for the implementation of this proposal, however, when added to the principle of justice prepaid by the citizen, it becomes an open and shut case.

Furthermore, the removal of oppressive taxation and the return of many private functions now performed, badly, by the State, will remove much of the cause of bitterness and resentment present in citizens, adding to the effect of decreasing both offences and litigation. For who has not seen an angered or frustrated person turning on someone (or the dog) who was an entirely innocent bystander?

Shakespeare was profoundly correct, *'Sparing justice feeds iniquity'*; so too Herbert Spencer, *'... most of the civil offences now committed, are committed **because** of the inefficiency of our present judicial system.'* Surely a free judicial service combined with the abolition of taxation would ensure that injuries wittingly committed would almost cease. We have a great deal to gain from a completely free judicial service and nothing to fear.

This is the third and final proposition of this book, a Free Judicial Service. The first proposal, the 'Single Tax', has had a populist phase in Henry George's time when his book *Progress and Poverty* sold in its millions. The second proposal, The Minimal State, limiting the State to defence and policing, has had periods of history when it virtually occurred and it is currently going through a period of theoretical popularity especially in the Libertarian movement in the U.S.A. The Free Judicial Service, however, has dawned on the consciousness of very few, and its implementation has yet to be written up in detail (the idea of a Public Defender is similar in concept). It is a principle of high order, which will one day come to be recognised. These three proposals together make up the Judicial State and form the thesis of this book.

The connection between revenue and fines

One of the most common methods of imposing a punishment upon a convict is to levy a fine, and this has as a side effect the raising of a certain amount of revenue for government. This necessary coincidence may be put to good use when we are faced with problems such as pollution with carbon dioxide in air and nitrogen in water supplies. In these cases the production of the pollutant is a by-product of the innocent use of natural resources for productive purposes. In these cases, judicial charges may be implemented on fossil fuels and nitrogenous fertilisers, with the revenue raised used directly to ameliorate the attendant pollution problems. In addition the charge will cause some reduction in use, and/or stimulate more efficient methods of use, and hence will reduce the pollution somewhat.

Something similar may be argued for a 'duty' on alcohol and tobacco, though only on the grounds of the impairment of the freedom and rights of others. The important point is that these and similar forms of taxation (and taxation is the correct word for it in these situations) should be part of the administration of justice and not part of revenue collection, as they are a form of fine for a diffuse infringement of the rights of others, and not, primarily, a revenue source.

We have now completed the outline of the functions of the State as follows: to raise revenue from the Single Tax on Land value; to provide

policing and defence forces; and to establish and administer a comprehensive legal and judicial service that is free to its citizens. This is the
Judicial State.

The structure of the Judicial State

We have traced, from principles of individual rights, the only legitimate
functions of the State. These are defence, police, and a judicial service
funded by a just revenue source. These are the only functions of the State
and it must desist from all other activities. So how is this State to be
constituted?

The separation of powers

Clearly in any State there is a need for some sort of board of management
(executive) which daily directs the forces of the State. From the 'Conflict
Theory' we can see that government originated from the use of force, and
we may note that the temptation of monopoly power would remain, even
in the Judicial State. Many States have been taken over at the instigation
of their own armed forces and there is thus a requirement for a system
of checks and balances within the State apparatus to guard against
such abuse.

The idea of dividing the powers of government into three parts, each
with some power over the other has been traced back to John Lilburne[12]
in a pamphlet of 1649, and others subsequently. Prior to this there had
been a separation of powers but it was between the Sovereign, the Lords
and the Commoners. Nowadays the separate powers are Legislature,
Executive and Judiciary.

The Legislature creates the laws and represents the people; its members
may be called the Representatives. The Executive carries out the day to
day work of the State: its policing and defence function; its handling of
potentially lethal and deadly force. The Judiciary decides legal cases.

The man most associated with the theory of the balance of powers
is Charles Louis Montesquieu who was born at La Brede, about ten
miles from Bordeaux, France in January 1689. His magnum opus, *The
Spirit of the Laws,* was brought out in 1748 and he died in February 1755
in Paris.

---

[12] See F.A. Hayek's *The Constitution of Liberty*, Chapter 11, note 56.

Montesquieu did not, however, produce a comprehensive account of the theory, and is indeed open to more than one interpretation in part of it. Nor has anyone else produced a definitive treatment of the issue. Montesquieu's general idea of a three part government, each with a measure of power over the others, has become widely acknowledged and has been practised with comparative success. His ideas have stood the test of time, and the limitations of the Judicial State do not materially alter his thesis.

The radical simplification entailed in the Minimal State theory would, however, change the *dynamics* of government. Particularly the deep-seated injustice in access to Land – which derived from the conflict between rulers and ruled, and which threw up class and party politics – would be eradicated. Thus we can anticipate that the legislature would no longer enshrine 'Opposition', but that all its members would cooperate to find the best possible legislation. There would be a common enemy, namely the evil in individuals, and all would be united to counter its actions.

So we need a body of elected representatives to enact legislation as well as a smaller executive body to carry out the day to day functions of governance. But how best to elect or select the people for each of these bodies? In the U.S.A., the election of the Legislature is entirely separated from the election of the President, who, when elected, goes on to select the rest of his executive team, while the British method is to have the Executive elected by and from the Legislature. There are significant problems with both these methods. The British fall foul of the very thing that Montesquieu warned about:

> ... if ... the executive power should be committed to a certain number of persons selected from the legislative body, there would be an end then of liberty; by reason the two powers would be united, as the same persons would sometimes possess, and would be always able to possess, a share in both.
>
> *The Spirit of the Laws*, Book XI, Section 6

The American system has problems of its own, firstly it involves the vast added expenditure of the Presidential election and, secondly, it frequently leads to an unbridgeable chasm between the Executive and the Legislature causing much friction and even stalemate. In fact, separate elections for the Executive and Legislature seem almost calculated to cause division between them and appear to be a flaw in the constitution of the U.S.A.

But there is a compromise between these two positions. If the President or Prime Minister is elected by and from the Legislature, but is then disqualified from direct participation in the Legislature, and can then select his team from within the Legislature or outside it, on the same condition that all Executive members be excluded from the Legislature.

This procedure for the establishment of the Executive would ensure that the relationship between the Executive and the Legislature would be both *sufficiently close*, ensuring a good working relationship (the Legislature having voted for the Executive head) and *sufficiently distant* (none of the Executive team could participate in the Legislature) ensuring that Montesquieu's fears, quoted above, would be groundless.

With the establishment of the Legislature and the Executive, it remains for the two of them to establish the Judiciary. The notion of nominations coming from the Executive but requiring the approval of the Legislature (as in the U.S.A.) may be as good as any other system. Once established, however, the Judiciary is allowed to get on with its job without interference from the Executive or Legislature. The only power retained by the Executive over the Judiciary is that of Impeachment. The Representatives and the Executives are subject to the Judiciary in the same manner as all other citizens. This is the balance of power.

The election procedure for representatives may change due to the radical changes in a Judicial State. Since the main function of the representatives is to be a channel of communication between the government and the citizens, and since we expect that there will be a radically different spirit within the Legislature – cooperation not confrontation – the 'first past the post' or the list system, with small, single-seat constituencies, might be more appropriate than proportional representation with large, multiple-seat constituencies. General elections may well be less frequent than today, again due to the non-confrontational nature of the legislature. We may also speculate that political parties would disappear – the best person for the job in each area being the only condition necessary for election as a Representative.

The background against which this tripartite government acts must be some form of fundamental law or constitution. The success of the much vaunted American constitution points to the importance of its existence, on the other hand the obvious failings of the U.S.A. may be due to the constitution's failure to respect the absolute right of citizens to the totality of their income and property; as well as its failure to protect common rights to Land.

The proposals above make little or no change in the relationship of the State in its external or foreign policies. Foreign relations will continue as before. It would seem likely that – as today – like-minded States would club together especially in the field of defence where great savings can be made by such cooperation. This would be especially true for Georgist, Minimal, Judicial States since the protection of their citizens is their sole *raison d'etre,* in fact we might almost consider foreign affairs to be a branch of the defence forces. The power of such States to make or break treaties with other States would remain as today, and of course they would still have to act within both their own constitution and legislation.

To sum up, the functions then of each branch are as follows:

1   The Legislature – to represent the citizens, to elect the Executive and to formulate, amend and retire legislation.
2   The Executive – to organise and fund the defence and police forces, as well as administering the treasury, the judicial system and foreign affairs.
3   The Judiciary – to decide in cases brought before it, using both constitutional and legislative law.

Internally there is a need for appropriately sized constituencies for electing the representatives, as well as similar court jurisdictions. The Representative for each district could work from a government owned office located centrally in the district when not working in the Legislature itself. This is the State: Georgist, Minimal and Judicial.

*

We have now come to the end of Part II of this book in which we have outlined three positive proposals for the transformation of the State so that it will leave the maximum power and freedom in the hands of its citizens. To recap, the three proposals and their rationale are as follows.

1   Raise all government revenue from a Single Tax on Land value and remove all taxes currently levied on Labour and Capital. The earth is the common property of all the planet's inhabitants, so exclusive access to any plot can only be had on payment of a market-determined ground rent to the communal body (the State) for the privilege. The returns to Labour and Capital investment are 100% private property so any tax, levy, excise or duty applied to them are theft, even if performed by the State.

2 The functions of the State are strictly limited to defence, policing and justice. The force that the State monopolises can only derive from the force that each individual has a natural right to use, so the State must be limited to doing only what individuals have the right to do. If you want to know if the State has the moral right to do something, you have to imagine you yourself taking a gun and forcing that action on your neighbours. Only if you believe you personally have that right then you have the right to expect the State to do it on your behalf.

3 The State must supply justice free to all its citizens who require it. No longer is there a cost for going to court. The State has appropriated your right to self-defence so must defend you without charging you.

PART III

The Functions of Society

CHAPTER 7

Life Without the State

*'To explain all nature is too difficult a task for any one man
or even for any one age. 'Tis much better to do a little
with certainty, and leave the rest for others that come
after you, than to explain all things.'*
Sir Isaac Newton

'What can we do to help business?'
Colbert (Minister of King Louis XIV)
'Laissez-nous faire.'
Legendre (Businessman)

THE MONOPOLY on force which defines the State can only be derived from the natural right of its citizens to self-defence; consequently that force may be used only in the defence of each and every citizen equally. This is the State's only legitimate role. This Law of the State – The Law of Legitimate Force – does not sit easily on the human psyche. For thousands of years, mankind has suffered under a State concept that has known few boundaries and which has successfully insinuated itself into almost every facet of individual life, from cradle to grave, womb to tomb. This monstrous State has so impressed itself into the human psyche that its diminution to nothing more than defence and justice leaves an enormous hole. How will life go on without it? Fear, panic and awe are the normal reactions of people so conditioned to the State's power and scope when presented with this idea. It is this conditioning that forms the greatest barrier to the removal of the State from all its inappropriate functions.

The three largest departments of the modern 'Welfare State', Health, Education and Welfare, along with Economic services, form the bulk of most State's spending, as well as forming the most frequent and intimate interactions with its citizens. The suggestion that the State simply withdraws from all these areas will have enormous impact on every citizen. And change, even if it is for the better, is not something that everyone can easily cope with. In fact it is the fear of the unknown (even if that unknown is a better life) that can paralyse and provoke resistance. This fear is the barrier to the Minimal State, the State confined to its proper functions.

Past discussions of such political Libertarianism have been handicapped by the continued (and unquestioned) injustices and disincentives enshrined in the revenue system that has been the norm for modern States as well as for proposed Minimal States. When, however, we take into consideration that power instantly reverts to the individual the moment that taxation is abolished, and that equal access to the earth's resources is provided by the Georgist revenue solution, the whole picture changes. So for the discussion of this chapter we assume that taxation has been abolished and the Georgist solution has been implemented. Our Minimal State is Georgist; uniquely so.

It may be said that State power comes out of the barrel of a gun, but really it comes from the products that such weapons plunder. Those products (food, clothing, money, arms, munitions etc.) are the real source of power, and they are all products of Labour. Power, by its nature, derives from the application of Labour (plus Capital) to the Earth's resources: State power comes from this same source. The modern State simply helps itself to the power of the individual through the taxes it imposes. At worst, the State is parasitic on the individuals and associations of individuals who cooperate to produce this power. At best, the State is symbiotic; that is where it confines itself to its proper functions, protecting its citizens from internal and external attack. Here the security provided by the State is a 'good' that increases the power and value of all that its citizens produce.

I am sure that the claim for a speedy doubling of the gross domestic product of any nation that introduces the Georgist solution will be treated with scepticism if not outright derision. If we claim that the benefit will be more in the order of a 20-30% increase, arguing that incentives to work will be so much increased and opportunities so vastly improved, maybe we will be believed. But I am not so sure that the first claim is not the more accurate. The Law of Property and the Law of the State – the Law of Legitimate Force – are natural Laws, like Gravitational, Aerodynamic, Electrical and Magnetic Laws. These are not toys. These are not the imagination of wild eyed revolutionaries. These are written into the warp and woof of the universe. To ignore them is to play with fire – those who play with fire get burnt, those who treat it with respect and learn to harness it gain immeasurably. I believe that the move to the Single Tax will harness a natural Law and lead to a quantum leap in the economic power of each citizen, and that would be so even if the State were to continue to spend in much the same fashion as it does today. What we are saying here is that on top of the Georgist solution, State expenditure can easily be curtailed by half or even two thirds, further empowering the citizen by a similar amount. Later in this chapter I will venture to speculate on some figures.

In order to get some idea of how power will return to the individual with the Georgist solution, we must consider the following. The Land Value Tax (Natural Resource Rent) will be purely market led. That is to say that the market will decide which sites are the most valuable, and which the least, and will give them a ranking order. It will therefore be impossible to under-utilise valuable Land (let alone hold it out of use), so optimal use will be made of each and every plot of Land. Site owners will have to make their sites pay the market rent so they will necessarily suck in Labour and Capital to make this happen. This effect will occur all across the nation, not on just one or two unused sites; it will initiate a major dynamic change in returns to Labour (and Capital). Instead of Labour competing to reduce wages to some survival minimum or legal minimum as happens now, site owners will compete for Labour driving up wages to their correct levels. The stimulus effects of the Georgist solution are both very powerful and fair. The State or nation that first goes Georgist will suck in Labour and Capital from all surrounding nations, until they too cop on and follow suit.

A recent TV program about a number of apprentices competing for one highly paid position has been very popular. The dynamic that makes the show click is the real life shortage of well-paid jobs and the threat of unemployment. This gives the boss his power and his punch-line: 'You're fired!' The Georgist solution reverses this dynamic completely. Instead of people competing for well-paid jobs, it will be well paid positions competing for appropriately skilled people. With good jobs easy to get, the line that will carry the same punch and power will be:

'I quit!' Employers and employees will be on an equal footing at least. At last.

At every point, from the raising of revenue to the delivery of its services, current State's systems are inefficient, wasteful and destructive. The way taxes are raised undermines the incentive of the taxpayer and creates unemployment. There are also collection costs and compliance costs to be paid. As money is passed from Revenue to the Spending departments more is used up in the process. Government spending then on these services itself increases the cost of them. Just because it is State money, pigs come to the trough not caring about how greedy they may appear. It is 'our' money after all; 'let me have my share!' Up goes the price.

The switch from State funded health, education, welfare and economic services to personal responsibility for these issues, involves a further dramatic win/win situation, due to the superior knowledge of the free market. Only at the level of the individual and the family is there full knowledge of the needs. The combination of everyone's need forms the 'market', this is what we mean when we say that the market knows what services are required. The State and its bureaucrats, no matter how well meaning, can never attain the knowledge of the market, they can only second guess it. Such second guesses can be wildly wrong. Faced with the choice of a new scanner for a hospital or thousands of prescriptions for the elderly, the bureaucrat has a 50% chance of getting it right; and a 50% chance of getting it wrong. The market, which signals through money spent by millions of autonomous individuals and families making their preferred choice, will get it right – every time. Such spending will be 100% efficient. State spending in this area may be only 50% efficient.

So, in addition to the empowerment of all citizens through the switch to the Single Tax, we now have the improved efficiency of individuals making their own choices about their own spending behaviour. Combining the Georgist proposal with the Minimal State we have a double win/win situation.

If we add up all the waste, destruction, and inefficiency of providing these services through the State, it may well be that €100 from the taxpayer provides only €50 of services. This halving of power, when reversed, becomes a doubling in power. So the removal of the State from health, welfare, education and economic services will allow – through reduced taxation – the individual and family room to provide for themselves far more efficiently. And this is on top of the increase in power returned to citizens through the Single Tax. This double return of power to the individual will be the filler for that hole we noted would be created in the human psyche by the withdrawal of the State from individual lives. But because this power is the true and natural source – while the State was but an imposter *'come only to steal, kill and destroy'* – the human psyche will know it as rain on a parched landscape. Lush growth and rich harvests will dull the memory of thousands of years of false and twisted nature.

If we examine the four big spending services separately, we can find further unique arguments in favour of their privatisation.

Economic services

State intervention to provide economic services such as development of industry, agriculture, manufacturing, technology or any other field, are usually justified as a way of reducing unemployment, poverty, under capitalisation or other similar rationales. The complete removal of taxes from Labour and Capital with the introduction of the Natural Resource Rent will completely transform the economic scene to such an extent that government involvement will become *unjustifiable* since there will be full employment, optimal Capital development and appropriate natural resource usage. Economic services will be the first area for State withdrawal. The private economy – that engine of capitalism – will immediately benefit from the proposed changes, particularly the abolition of taxes. The only tears that will be shed with the passing of State involvement here are those shed into the champagne glasses of those celebrating their economic growth under a tax free society. Cheers Crocodiles!

Education

The State is a bureaucratic, hide-bound organisation by nature and can never react to changes in technology and society as fast as they happen. Education is a case in point. The age of computers and the internet has opened a new chapter in the history of information such that some are calling it the Information Age. The virtually instant access to information from any modern household dramatically changes the dynamics of schooling and education. Lifelong learning is now a practical reality. Individuals can take spells in productive jobs alternating with time out for further education followed by better or more satisfying work. It is no longer so important that a child 'completes' his/her education by a certain age. With full employment the economic norm, the stress will be off the pupil to achieve. Education will be more like breathing or laughing or playing. Other values, such as how one treats fellow pupils and teachers, will become more important. Early school leavers may go to jobs that require manual and artistic skills that cannot be taught in schools. The appalling double waste represented by unemployed college graduates on State welfare will become history. Privatised education will mean a whole range of tools, from home schooling, private schools and colleges, to on-the-job training, apprenticeships and scholarships funded by industries requiring certain skills. With full employment and high wages, families will easily be able to afford the courses that they choose for both their children and themselves.

Healthcare

We have already discussed the problem of the State trying to assess needs for healthcare and to ration scarce resources amongst competing require-ments. We can also ask the question: How much of modern dis-ease is actually caused by injustices of the modern economic system, the system propagated by the current State? Modern medicine has surprised itself with the discovery of strong links between psychology and disease. The chance of a cancer victim beating the disease is remarkably linked to the attitude of the individual. A positive, hopeful attitude leads to life, whereas depression and gloom tend toward death. Many other studies show the same thing. 'A cheerful heart is good medicine' indeed.

Due to the State's theft of much private income, many are driven to poverty and despair knowing that they have been wronged but unable to understand how or why, or by whom. How much mental and physical disease is the result? How many turn to drugs, legal and illegal, to dull the pain? The excitement and drive that belongs to a man with a vision to better himself and his family also keep him sane and healthy, for this is why he was created. To dream, to plan, to achieve – to make mistakes and learn from them – these are all part of the fulfilment that makes a person whole, but they are impossible under life controlled by the State.

We noted earlier that the taxation of Labour places an unwarranted premium on 'time' – whether our own time or anybody's time – and this is factored into our subconscious thinking about how fast we need to achieve every task, and it accelerates our fast paced lives; this is a source of constant and massive stress. Stress not only is the cause of much sickness but is frequently deadly; the removal of taxes from Labour will thus de-stress society leading to much greater health for everyone. The removal of taxation and State meddling from everyday life will have enormous benefits for the health of its citizens. This in turn will reduce health requirements which will therefore become more affordable. So health services (or insurance) will be easily affordable in the prosperous and fair Georgist economy.

Welfare

The current State, through the disincentive effects of its taxation of production and its legal support of Land speculation and resource monopolisation, is easily the single largest cause of poverty and need for welfare. Unemployment and poverty are the direct results of its vicious actions and inactions. The Georgist solution turns back the tide on all this and allows freely cooperating people to produce all the bounty that nature has to offer, ensuring at the same time that this bounty is distributed fairly – to each according to effort and ability. As already noted, property owners will compete to drive up wages rather than Labour competing to drive them down. True, the poor will always be with us, but occasionally and sporadically, not epidemically or in plague proportions. Welfare was originally an individual affair run by community organisations, and these will be well able to cope when the economy functions as it should. There will be both a reduced need for charity and an increased ability to give.

The dynamic created by the faceless, nameless State handing out welfare is poisonous. Recipients do not feel the gratitude or sense of responsibility which exists when charity is given privately, out of a generous heart. In many cases the warmth and love that goes along with private charity is the real need; this is a need that the State can never fulfil. The lonely widowed pensioner who goes once a week to the local welfare office to collect enough to exist for another week is a creation of a perverse, uncaring 'welfare' State. It is the State that has burdened him and his family for a lifetime with its taxation, and has fenced him off from opportunity (with its lack of a Land Value Tax) resulting in his deprived state. His family also struggle to make ends meet so they are restricted in their ability to give him the financial and human support he needs and which they have a natural desire to give.

The above is yet another cogent argument for the Georgist solution, and this should not be a surprise for if it is truly a genuine solution, there will be many such arguments. But there is the further argument that State welfare actually creates welfare dependants. Because there is no obligation created by a faceless and nameless benefactor, some welfare recipients feel that they have a right to the welfare and are not willing to use the talents that they do possess to support themselves. Some, in fact, use amazing natural talents and gifts to increase their welfare take – talents that would otherwise be put to good use in a productive life are employed to milk the State. Some take this 'career' even further by supplementing this free income with a life of crime. How many criminals are supported by State welfare? The devil finds work for idle hands. State welfare creates welfare needs, so the removal of State welfare, along with the implementation of the Georgist solution, will reduce welfare needs to levels that are easily taken care of by individuals and voluntary charitable associations. Crime levels will drop dramatically as the State will no longer support this brand of criminal.

It is not long in terms of human history that the State has involved itself in the provision of health, welfare, education and economic services; two or three hundred years only. Once the will is present, it will not take much time for the situation to be returned to where it once was. All these services began as private and voluntary initiatives – many as functions of the church. The exact path required to make the return journey is not tricky or difficult and much has already been written about it under the topic of privatisation. If the withdrawal is announced in advance, if it is well thought through and it ensures that incentives match power returned, and with the right political will, there is no reason why the whole change could not be achieved in a generation or less, five to twenty years. Badly handled it could take longer. However long, it will be change for the better, truly a silk purse from a sow's ear!

Thus far I have presented the three main proposals of this book on a foundation of natural, inalienable rights inherent in all individuals. These things should be done because they are the right things to do; but they will also have major economic repercussions by which they may also be justified. We live in an age of economic measurement, where many ask questions such as how much better off will individuals or the whole nation be if we follow this or that proposal. To answer such questions we must first issue a caveat: we must admit that even very generalised figures are simply speculation and could be out by many percentage points, but the direction to which these figures point will be correct. Also we have the difficulty of measuring the effects, given that the transformation will take years to accomplish, 5 years or more maybe. If we say that for a particular nation the overall effect will be a 50% economic improvement we would expect to see annual growth rates in the order of 10 % for a number of years then settling down to an unrelenting 3 or 4%, but how much of that 10% was due to our changes and how much to natural growth would likely be debated for ever. But we can be confident of the trends.

All three of our proposals target personal incentives. The Single Tax will vastly incentivise the work ethic while placing resources in the hands of those who will use them best. The Minimal State will, by returning all the decisions to the individuals who will be spending their own money, lead to the wisest and most economic spending on health, education and welfare. The Judicial State will incentivise the greatest respect for the property, life and liberty of others. How much each of these will add in economic terms may be largely guesswork, but it will most certainly be 'add' and not 'subtract'.

I still hesitate to put figures on these proposals but will do so to give some idea of the economic directions we can expect. I have sought throughout this book to argue the benefits with words, not maths, and I rest my case on rights, logic and argument. But for those who need figures – no matter how speculative – here goes:

Single Tax economic boost

If we consider a typical western nation which takes 35% of all wealth in taxes on Labour and Capital as government revenue, this amounts to a stupendously large 'fine' on production and this would be eliminated. All wages and salaries would become 'cash in hand'; there would be no 'employment tax' on companies offering jobs; no tax on Capital gains or trading. The market would be totally fluid. Economic gain 20%. The business of Land speculation would be totally destroyed by the Land tax ensuring all valuable Lands and resources are brought into use; under-utilised lands would be brought to best use. Economic gain 10%. Together these two would also have synergistic gains, say 5% more, so the total economic gain from the Single Tax change 35%.

Minimal State economic boost

Given that some 30% of GDP currently being spent by bureaucrats on health, education and welfare will be returned to individuals to spend for themselves, which may lead to a 50% improvement in spending, then the gain will be half of 30% which is 15%.

Free judicial service economic benefit

The free judicial service will lead to greatly increased respect for the persons and property of others and therefore reduce crime and theft. But is it possible to measure? The generation of full employment will remove temptation to 'idle hands', boosting the economy (counted under the Single Tax above) but also reduces the negatives of theft and crime. We could argue for a 5% economic benefit but since this is the one proposal where State spending will increase, we will allocate a zero net economic gain.

Combining the first two above, 35% gain from the Single Tax with a 15% gain from the Minimal State we reach a total of 50% overall gain.

Another question is how evenly these benefits will be distributed. If we carry on with our example above where the Gross Domestic Product (GDP) increases by 50% due to our proposals, what are the outcomes for the various economic sectors: those suffering severe hardship; those struggling to make ends meet; those 'happy with what we've got but sure would appreciate more'; those who have all they need, and then those who have no idea what to do with all they have got! The first thing we can be clear about is that these benefits will be greatest for those who are poorest and will diminish proportionately as we ascend the economic levels. Let us take someone who is on State welfare and just around the poverty level; their transition to a job which pays the same as the State hand-out represents a 100% increase since that person is now contributing to society and not taking from it (this is in addition to the self-esteem and respect from others he/she may feel). But as discussed elsewhere, jobs would no longer trend towards a basic minimum, but reach a respectful self-sustaining norm. Say this were twice the poverty level, now the individual in question going from State welfare to a decent job represents 200% improvement in position. For those currently on minimum wages their incomes may double which gives a 100% increase. Those on good salaries will also see healthy improvements but at a more modest level and even the top earners can expect to see some gains provided that their incomes are not derived from Land speculation. To sum up we can say that the least well off will benefit most, but not at the expense of the rich for they too will see gains.

Monopoly services

We have thus far not considered the other functions traditionally undertaken by governments such as the provision of roads, money, banking, water supply and other similar services. These are far trickier and more problematic to deal with. Many of these have been State functions since the dawn of the civilisation. Here we encounter a problem of a different order.

We began this work building up the thesis that the only legitimate functions of the State are defence, police and justice, and we have discussed how the majority of current State expenditure may be privatised without problems. We are then left with an apparently miscellaneous list of services that our theory says should be privatised also. This list includes roads, bridges, piers, harbours, mail, telephone, water, sewerage, refuse collection, gas reticulation, parks and beaches, buses and trains. How these are treated vary from State to State and in some there has been a move toward privatisation in recent years.

Two exceptions stand out within this group and will be treated in the next chapter, these are Money and Banking. The rest I propose to treat as a generalised group. Though some of these services have been privatised recently, e.g. water and telephones, there is only one school of thought – the Anarcho-Capitalists – that wholly and completely espouses private enterprise in the supply of all. Even Bastiat, whose anti-State logic is most rigorous, said that the State must administer what he called 'public property', in which he included roads and rivers.[13]

The fact that some of the above services have already been privatised, and that many of the others have been partly 'contracted out' to free enterprise companies indicates that the Anarcho-Capitalists may well be correct; even with respect to the provision of roads. The principle from which we started, and which Bastiat so strongly espoused (that, because law is force, it may only perform those functions where force is legitimate among individuals) indicates that all these services should indeed be private sector. This principle has not, in these cases, been

---

[13] See 'Public and Private Services', an essay in the collection *Economic Harmonies*, published by the Foundation for Economic Education Inc., 1964.

superseded by any greater. The fact that a large measure of the road service has developed at the behest of force (the tax-master's route to the 'cows' he milks) does not mean that it could not have developed from the free cooperation of citizens, or that it may not one day be organised by such cooperation. Actually, much of the road service is still developed and maintained privately or semi-privately through the cooperation of individuals and companies, in new developments and in remote areas.

The relatively small portion of present State expenditure on all these 'monopoly' functions – in Ireland it is about 5% – and the large degree of controversy over their position, makes the necessity for dealing conclusively with this subject small. Indeed the reforms of this thesis are sufficiently large that we can safely leave the reforms of 'monopoly services' to the next generation, who, being brought up in a free enterprise culture with equal rights of all to the Land, and living under a judicial service which truly ensures Justice among men, will doubtless arrive at a satisfactory solution.

We might, however, get a glimpse of the possibility for the provision of roads (which are probably the trickiest in theory) through private enterprise, if it is considered that in Ireland some years ago the State collected 40% more in road fuel taxes than it expended on roads (1988: £Ir.500m revenue; £Ir.300 spent). A private road company might therefore collect its fees by allowing only vehicles with duty-paid fuel to use its roads; and that duty could be much lower than the present fuel taxes. Provided that the law upholds the right of the company to so limit the access of vehicles, such a scenario might indeed work.

The enormous cooperation of men in the attainment of unselfish aims that exists today, in a situation where a large proportion of private means is forcibly removed – and largely wasted – and where justice is rarely done among men, indicates the potential for future cooperation. In a society where power is returned wholesale to individuals, and where true justice is universally enforced by the State, cooperation will have to be experienced to be believed. The limits then of voluntary association would lie only in the combination of natural Law and the human imagination. Those who feel strongly about something can get together with those who are like minded and together work towards their ends, such as taking care of those in need or saving a unique wildlife area, or exploring the universe or sending a man to Mars. The State can only be an impartial observer in these areas.

For those who think that the absence of the force of law would mean that in rare cases, an encounter with an unreasonable and uncooperative individual would bring about stalemate, it must be noted that there are two powerful forms of social persuasion which have a great record of success though sometimes used for unworthy causes. These persuaders – boycotting, and sending to Coventry – are tools which may be harnessed through voluntary cooperative organisation without the use of force. And the result, too, may be much more socially positive. Instead of the uncooperative individual ending up a bitter complier, or a prisoner of the legal system, social pressure may actually lead to a real change of heart especially when his capitulation results in his genuine restoration to social life.

The Judicial State not only allows for, but actually encourages, greater cooperation of individuals and voluntary organisations. Only under such a regimen will we see what human social life truly means.

To sum up, the functions of society are: *all those things that lie outside the functions of the Judicial State, everything other than Defence, Police and Justice.*

The inevitable impact of a discussion about the removal of the State from various areas of life will undoubtedly be negative because we are proposing an undoing of something existing; and that is negative. We need to balance this impact by focusing thoughts on the positive: what will the voluntary (profit making and non-profit) organisations look like that will rise up to take over those functions relinquished by the State? We already have many of them in existence today but they will become more powerful and important as the State is pruned back to size.

There exists a certain body of writing in the Classical Liberal/ Libertarian tradition, of how society would function under a Minimal State, although it has largely been written without consideration of zero production taxes, equal access to Land and a free Judicial Service. Of all writers, Herbert Spencer comes closest to a full discussion of this topic; his *The Man versus the State* and *Social Statics* are particularly exhaustive, but somewhat dated. Frank McEachran's *Freedom the only End* is outstanding, being beautifully poetic and inspiring, full of vision and hope, while providing an historical and philosophical viewpoint. Albert J. Nock's, *Our Enemy the State*, is incisive and historical but, sadly, despairs of hope.

In this chapter we have examined how society will perform those functions which the State has wrongly assumed and which it so ineffi- ciently performs, how individuals and free associations of individuals will take over and perform flawlessly and without apparent effort (think the development of the smart phone) in a truly free market. The only area we did not consider is the area of Money supply and Banking; this is the subject of the next chapter.

CHAPTER 8

Money, Banking and the Trade Cycle

'History does not repeat itself, but it rhymes.'
Mark Twain

'Let money be your measure, not your ruler.'
Anon

T HE LOGIC of the Minimal State, that States may do only those things that are legitimately performed by force, means that governments have no direct role in money or banking. Indirectly, by enforcing the law of contract, the State does play an important supporting role but that is simply the outworking of its monopoly on force. The Minimal State can have no direct role in money and banking; these are completely within the domain of the free market. Period.

The trouble with this statement is that it flies in the face of a virtual global monopoly of State currency and centralised State banking systems which started about 140 years ago, becoming almost universal today. Furthermore, both academic theory and common perception support the practice; indeed, after the latest banking failures in 2008/9 there were loud public cries for the last remaining vestige of free enterprise in this sector – the commercial banks – to be nationalised. To make the argument for 'laissez-faire' banking, where free enterprise not only chooses its own currency, but also creates it, might appear to be an overwhelming task, however, a dispassionate look at the history and origin of money and banking reveals that they are totally free market creatures, robust enough to survive for centuries on end but die immediately upon capture by the State. The State mimic can serve the market well enough but it lacks the extraordinary flexibility and magical quality of the original wild creature.

On the personal level, money can be a hard thing to balance and is often a hard thing to discuss dispassionately. To those who do not have enough, it can become a matter of desperation, to those who have more than enough, it can become a heady drug, fuelling a lust for more and more. However, the amount that is enough is very different for different people, so how do we frame our discussion? The wisest words on this subject that I can find are from Austrian economist Hans F. Sennholz in his *Money and Freedom*, 1985.

> There is no absolute monetary stability, never has been, and never can be. Economic life is a process of perpetual change. People continually choose between alternatives, attaching ever-changing values to economic goods; therefore, the exchange ratios of their goods are forever adjusting. Since nothing is fixed, nothing can be measured. Economists searching for absolute stability and measurement are searching in vain, and they become disruptive and potentially harmful to the economic well-being of society when they call upon government to apply its force to achieve the unattainable.
>
> Money is no yardstick of prices. It is subject to man's valuations and actions in the same way that all other economic goods are. It is subjective, as well as objective. Exchange values continually fluctuate and, in turn, affect the exchange ratios of other goods at different times and to different extents. There is no true stability of money … There is no fixed point or relationship in economic exchange.

The modern era of centralised fractional reserve banking based on legal tender currency arose out of fractional reserve banking relying on gold-backed fiduciary (free-enterprise) money. The reasons given for this change were the episodic and regular failures of this free market money/banking system. To discuss this we first need to understand what real, free-market money is. Actually there are two; the first is commodity money, in particular precious metals such as gold and silver, but it can be almost anything that is of regular quality and reasonably long lived. Primitive peoples use stone, beads, cattle or other livestock, schoolboys use glass 'marbles', wartime conditions relied on cigarettes, brandy or ladies stockings among other things, frontiersmen turned to animal pelts and whisky, while agricultural grains help out farming communities.

In the long run and on a global range, the free market ultimately settles on the precious metals; these are the quintessential commodity moneys.

The second form of free market money is credit, particularly in the written form, so it is credit money or credit notes. It is within the power of any individual to grant credit to another, friends and family often do it on an informal basis. When this credit becomes written down and a legally binding contract is made, then a form of money has been created, however clumsy and un-versatile it may be. Business invoices not yet paid are an example of this. The next step in making this free market credit into real money is for an intermediary to step in and broker the credit transaction. This leads to free-market issued notes (fiduciary notes) and a free market banking system.

The third form of money is not free market but State money which exists by State decree, so it is 'fiat' money, but that is too honest a word for today so we call it 'legal tender'. This money can be used by the free market if it is well managed but its very existence depends on the outlawing of the real thing.

The era of 'laissez-faire' banking or 'free' banking (the era before the current one) began when goldsmiths who, in addition to their primary trade, also took in precious metals in all forms for safe keeping. For this service they charged their customers and of course gave a receipt for the goods lodged, the receipt being a type of Credit or Fiduciary Note. To begin with these notes were issued to named individuals but soon it was found that they were more useful if made out to 'the bearer' as this enabled them to pass from hand to hand and so they became 'currency'. It was so much easier to make payments with these receipts – rather than carry around weights of precious metals – that gradually they were less and less often cashed in; they simply went round and round as the equivalent weight of the metal they specified. Still today the English use a word for their currency that is the same as a unit of weight: the pound.

The fact that these deposit receipts became acceptable currency, and were seldom returned to the goldsmith for redemption, gave a unique opportunity for the smiths to issue identical notes that they could loan out at interest, using the gold in their vault as backing. Since both the original notes and the copies were seldom cashed in, with careful management, the goldsmith-turned-banker could be confident of having enough gold to meet any rare requirements for the metal. These early bankers thus could make money both ways, charging for safekeeping as well as charging for loans – but not for long. The invisible hand of competition once again moves and bankers begin to pay depositors to lodge metal in their vaults, so now they can only make on the difference between the interest they pay 'depositors' and the interest they charge on loans. And so it continues with modern banking today.

It may rightly be noted that during the period of transition, when bankers were charging customers a fee for safekeeping the gold and at the same time making interest bearing loans on the strength of the gold stored, they were behaving deceitfully and their actions were illegitimate. But that all changed when, instead of charging for safekeeping, they begin to pay to have other people's gold in their vaults, and when it becomes common knowledge that they loan out more notes than they have gold equivalent. The enormous improvement in convenience for traders to carry paper notes rather than to carry physical gold is worth the price, in which all sides take the risk of a run on the bank when notes are returned in excess of gold in the vault. All three parties, the owner of the gold, the banker and the borrower, all gain from this new development. The owner now receives interest instead of having to pay for safekeeping. The banker gets paid from the interest on the extra loans he can make, and the borrower benefits from cheaper and more available loans. Truly convenient money has been born and modern banking along with it. These gold backed notes were the final development of the free market banknote.

The more acceptable these banknotes became as currency, the less frequently they were cashed in. As the banker issued more loans, he could decrease the rate to the borrower and/or increase it to the depositor. The amount of gold (now called specie) in reserve became a fraction of the banknotes in circulation. This lead to the name Fractional Reserve Banking, which at its high water mark had gold reserve levels as low as 2% while still functioning properly. Banking crises (including runs on banks) did occur but that is not a problem unique to this style of banking. The modern central banking system is run on a completely different form of currency and yet suffers from similar or worse problems than this free-banking system just described.

This laissez-faire banking was practiced in places as diverse as Scotland, Australia, England, Sweden, China, France, Spain, Italy, Canada, South Africa, New Zealand, as well as some States of the U.S.A. In addition to this wealth of experience, the theory of 'Free Banking' has taken great strides recently, and a strong consensus has developed concerning the self-regulating mechanisms inherent within such a system. Theory shows that (contrary to popular expectation) a system where private enterprise (banking) has the power to print money leads to a strong and stable currency, one that is completely in tune with the needs of the market. It does not lead to inflation or unwarranted power for the banking sector; the 'magic' of competition ensures that this is so.

Unfortunately the State saw that control of the currency would greatly enhance its power, so as soon as a scheme could be hatched that allowed the State to produce a mimic currency and as soon as an excuse could be found to bring it into reality, it happened. By implementing legal tender laws – thus creating Fiat currency – and by centralising the banking system so that only one, politically controlled bank could issue the notes, it was done. The previously private, note-issuing banks now became private, note-distributing banks, dependent on the central bank for all issues. Now the State had such absolute control over the money supply that it would satisfy the dreams of tyrants – and where tyrants arise, as in Zimbabwe recently, it does. Otherwise it can work with reasonable effectiveness except for its tendency to inflation (or occasionally deflation) and its tendency to periodic banking crises and crashes.

This State-controlled banking system is called Centralised Fractional Reserve Banking and is practiced by almost all nations of the world. This is the banking system that so disastrously crashed in 2008/9, and was only kept afloat by government inputs stolen from the long suffering, wool-blinded taxpayer. Supporters of the present system suggest that fractional reserve banking on fiduciary currency (private banking on privately issued notes) was even less stable and more prone to crashing. A recent study, however, by George Selgin, *Bank Deregulation and Monetary Order* (Routledge Press, 1996), in which he compares failures of the banking system before and after the introduction of central banking shows clearly that the latter is worse than the former. Free(er) banking is in fact more stable than central banking.

The real issue is that all banking is notoriously prone to instability, and has been since its inception. Kevin Dowd in his *Laissez Faire Banking* (Routledge, 1993), devotes one chapter to a study of the (relatively) free-banking period of Australia. In it he recounts how the system worked brilliantly until the great Land price bubble of the 1880s which burst in October 1888 leading to a financial crash in 1889-90. Dowd's analysis focuses on how this crash was used as an *excuse* by the State to introduce central banking since it was not strictly the banks that collapsed but other property and Land based financial institutions that failed. In this he is correct but he misses the more important point which was clearly visible in this Australian example: no matter what the system of banking, it can never be stable if the Land price bubble is allowed to inflate and burst, because, inevitably Land prices insinuate themselves into the vaults of the banking system causing failures hard on the heels of the Land price crash. The Land price bubble is the heart of banking failures.

Phillip Anderson, in his recent book, *The Secret Life of Real Estate: How it moves and why* (Shepheard-Walwyn, 2008), makes a thorough survey of financial crises suffered by the U.S.A. since 1800, paying particular attention to the price of Land. Anderson demonstrates that a remarkably consistent cycle appears with a periodicity of about eighteen years. This is for recessions with a clear connection to the peaking and falling of Land values. His study shows eight clear examples of a banking crisis following hard on the heels of a crash in Land values.

1818	Peak in Federal Land sales.
1819	Bank failures and recession.
1836	Second quarter. Peak of Federal Land sales.
1837	May. Financial panic after multiple bank failures.
1854	Activity in Land market peak.
1857	September. Bank failures and financial panic.
1873	Summer. Land Values peak.
1873	September. Banks and stock market collapse.
1888	Federal Land sales peak.
1890	Land boom peaks.
1893	Bank failures peak.
1914	War interrupts cycle.
1927	The Great Real Estate crash.
1929	Stocks crash, the first recession since all Federal lands appropriated. This is why it was so bad; 4,800 banks fail due to exposure to the real estate bubble.
1930	Government close every bank in the nation for a period. The Fed fails to print sufficient money. Deflation reaches 25% in some years.
1943	War interrupts cycle.

1955   Land prices bottom out.

1974   Land values peak and banks fail simultaneously. REITs (Real Estate Investment Trusts) were the main vehicle for transmission of Land value into the financial system.

1989   Land Values peak.
1990/91 Banking crisis. Savings and Loans debacle.

To all these, we may now add:

2006/7 Land Values peak.
2008/9 Banking crisis and failures.

Philip Anderson also gives us the example of the 1996 peak of Land values in the Asian Tiger nations followed by their 1997 financial crash.

Japan is one of the few economies where Land prices are well monitored; they peaked in 1998. Wikipedia says that the highest price in central Tokyo at that time was US$ 1 million per square metre. Five years later it had declined by 99%; that it to say it was now valued at only $10,000 per square metre ($40 million per acre). Advisor to the Bank of Japan, Kazuo Ueda, in a paper at www.bis.org/publ/plcy07q.pdf sites this Land price crash as cause of the failure of the banking system for most of the nineties, and the continuing stagnation of the Japanese economy.

How many more examples are needed to make the point? When will the banking authorities wake up to the fact that this industry can only ever hope to be stable when Land prices are stable over time, and this is only possible when there are no taxes on Labour and Capital, and all government revenue is raised from Land Value Taxation? *The Single Tax is absolutely essential to a stable financial system.*

The true tragedy of the latest banking system failure will be if the causal link is not made and a future repeat is allowed to take place. There is only one sure way of preventing a future Land price crash from causing a collapse in the banking system (whatever type of banking system) and that is to prevent a Land price bubble from ever occurring again. And there is only one sure way of doing that: raise all revenue from Land values and abolish all taxes on Labour and Capital. Those who do not learn from history are bound to repeat it.

Central banking on Fiat money (the system we have today) turns out to be not only unstable and liable to systemic failure, but is historically inflationary with anything from 2% to 20%, and, under certain conditions can be hyper-inflationary. Central banking was introduced in a supposed effort to create a better banking system. The experiment that has lasted over a hundred years has clearly failed and it is now time to learn the big lesson. Private banks with rights to create money – laissez-faire banking – provide a sounder and more stable financial system; one to which we must return. But now we can see that by adopting the Single Tax we can, not just return to a better system, but we can look forward to one many times better than any previous when we remove the 'boat-rocking' power of Land price instability.

The withdrawal of the State from involvement in money and banking is not difficult or problematic. Other writers such as George Selgin have given full details of the steps required for laissez-faire banking to take over from Central banking. To summarise, these boil down to two steps: firstly, allowing private banks to issue their own banknotes; and, secondly, repealing legal tender laws. To these I would add a third: replacing all taxes on Labour and Capital with the Land Value Tax. The free market invented and developed both money and banking in the first place so there is no reason why the free market cannot once again resume this role, and perform it so much better than the State has ever done, or could ever do it.

The trade cycle and how the banking system became the catalyst for the boom and bust of Land prices.

There is no consensus in modern economics as to the cause of the trade cycle. In fact the 'dismal science' has almost no consensual agreements – it is usually 'on the one hand, and, on the other hand' – amazingly, however, there is agreement on the proposal that a Land tax will not distort trade. Henry George wrote his bestseller, *Progress and Poverty*, as a *journalist's* attempt at an *'inquiry into the cause of industrial depressions ...the remedy'*. Henry George saw and experienced the end of the first trade cycle in California when the continuous boom of the economy abruptly ended with the appropriation of all common Land. The periods of depression and expansion which follow each other regularly, was explained by George in a short contribution written by him in *Once a Week*, in 1894. The article was subsequently published as a pamphlet titled *Causes of Business Depression*. To quote the penultimate paragraph:

At the close of the last great depression (1879), I made an 'Examination of the Cause of Industrial Depression' in a book better known by its main title, *Progress and Poverty*, to which I would refer the reader who would see the genesis and course of business depressions fully explained. But their cause is clear. Idle acres mean idle hands, and idle hands mean a lessening of purchasing power on the part of the great body of consumers that must bring depression to all business. *Every great period of land speculation that has taken place in our history has been followed by a period of business depression, and it always must be so.* [Emphasis added.]

George's point is that it is the withdrawing of Land (the passive economic component) from the productive process which causes a dislocation of Labour and its product Capital (the two make up the active economic component), and removes it, the active component, from the source and basis for all productive effort. As the passive is withdrawn from the active partner, by the process of Land speculation during the boom periods, there eventually arrives a time when production and consumption are sufficiently choked to provoke a recession or depression. Few people have ever seen such a stark contrast as the first depression that ended the apparently endless boom of newly opened Lands, but George saw it take place in California, 'the land of opportunity'. He saw the first beggars appear and he made the connection with the barbed wire fences that prevented those very men reaching that Land. But in subsequent booms and busts it is not so clear cut: Land is both speculated on and underutilised, both leading to the fencing out of Labour. Even amongst tall buildings, intensive farming and mushrooming new housing, Land is invisibly withdrawn from Labour until the system breaks down and crashes.

George is correct in that this is the *primary* cause of recessions and depressions but his explanation misses out the enormously powerful magnifying effect of the expansion of the money supply which takes place on the back of the rise of Land values that accompanies the boom/speculation. Both the consumer and the producer expand their operations (consumption and production) against the value of their Land holdings, with the assistance of the banking system. Trade becomes manic as the treadmill of the boom becomes faster and faster until finally the steam that is inflating the Land price runs out and it has nowhere to go except down. As Land prices were going up, everyone with even the smallest holding felt they were getting richer by the week and could keep the purse strings loose. Then the Land prices slide and the feeling is of getting poorer, and so the purse strings are tightened with a consequent tightening of credit.

This turning point in the price of Land is a crucial one, one day the price is rising, and the next it is declining. This may seem strange but is clearly explained by Mason Gaffney in his paper 'The Great Crash of 2008'.

> The *rise* of Land prices cannot simply flatten out at a high plateau, because the *increment* has become part of the expected return for which purchasers pay and on which lenders rely. So prices that cannot rise further have to drop: there is no equilibrium level.

We have already noted the connection between the Land price bubble bursting globally in 2007 and the economic crash and financial crash which followed, and that this is a mirror image of Australia 1888-90 which we discussed earlier. To these we may add Japan in the early 1990s which clearly shows a boom and bust in Land value immediately prior to a banking crisis so severe that the economy has not been the same since. Japan is one of the few nations that meticulously records Land prices, so we do not have to rely on anecdotal evidence, the records are there for anyone to see. But the reason that Japan is still in the economic doldrums almost two decades later is that Land prices were not allowed to fall to their natural, market clearing level. Both the banking industry and Land prices have been artificially propped up by a series of blind governments, and this gives us a very important lesson for the global economy post 2009. Land prices must be allowed to return to a realistic level, one that is affordable for first time home owners and new generation entrepreneurs. Toxin-riddled banks must be allowed to go under. Better to have a serious 'clean out' of the system than to allow chronic indigestion for the next twenty years. Iceland has gone down this route and as a result it is returning to growth ahead of the rest of Europe.

We can now see that the so-called 'trade cycle' is really the penalty we suffer for a foolish and inefficient revenue system. Raise revenue without taxation and the economy will blossom and flourish in the continuous powerful pattern of a tropical forest, not that of a temperate cyclical one. Never again need there be calls for government to prime the economic pump, or to cool an overheated economy, or get at all involved in economic management. Like the tropical forest that needs only man's respect and admiration, the economy will flourish as its creator intended.

Conclusions

We can summarise then: in spite of common perception and ivy encrusted academics, money and banking can be left in the hands of private enterprise – there is a solid history of successful operation and a sound theory of why it works – indeed it is likely to be much safer than at present. The only State functions here are:

1   The removal of legal tender laws and other legal restrictions on banking.
2   The rigorous enforcement of the laws of contract through the free judicial service.
3   The collection of the Single Tax.

Running a central bank may take only a tiny fraction of 1% of government energy, with almost negligible cost but its importance to the discussion of this book lies in the fact that 100% of the revenue and expenses of the State as well as most of the innumerable transactions among individuals and companies in day to day life are made in the currency it creates. The importance of having the best possible money and banking system is therefore paramount. We must never again have banking and financial failures like 2008/9 – and now we don't have to!

Such is the importance of money and banking that there are some who believe that the abolition of central banking, and the return to free banking *alone* will suffice to flatten out the trade cycle. Such is the view of the Austrian school but, as we have noted above, the potential for speculation in Land must also be removed in order to eliminate the booms and busts of the trade cycle.

*

For further details of how money and banking works without the State see:

George Selgin, *The Theory of Free Banking*, 1988.
Kevin Dowd, *Laissez Faire Banking*, 1993.
George Selgin, *Bank Deregulation and Monetary Order*, 1996.

PART IV

Moral and Practical Issues

CHAPTER 9

Heaven on Earth

'God has given man two books: Holy Writ and nature.'

Galileo Galilei

IN HIS BOOK, *On Classical Liberalism and Libertarianism* (St. Martin's Press, 1987), Norman Barry points to an apparent conflict between the selfish impulses which drive commerce – and the libertarian order – and the received tradition of western morality ('Western morality' is Barry-speak for Judeo-Christian tradition or, more bluntly, Biblical morality). If Barry is correct, this conflict is sufficient to prevent all advances towards the Minimal State, and, as it represents the conclusion of a deeply incisive treatise on the subject, it must be taken very seriously.

Let us examine what Barry is saying:

> However, the difficulty libertarians have had in persuading others of the virtues of the system of liberty and spontaneity partly lies in the fact that the doctrine appears to be, and quite often is, in direct conflict with the received tradition of western morality. This tradition seems to urge a morality which obliges self-restraint not merely in those areas which require us to recognise the rights of others but also in actions which lead to purely self-fulfilment even though they do not abrogate or abridge such rights. In other words, this tradition understands moral perfection in terms of the sacrifice of personal values on behalf of the values of others.
>
> It is for this reason that the ethical biography of 'capitalism' appears as a morally tainted story; its economic success is said to be paid for in terms of a loss in morality precisely because the mechanisms (for example, selfishness and an allegedly uncaring competitive impulse) that drive the

economic system are successful to the extent that they violate western moral orthodoxy …

It is one of the tasks of a completed system of libertarian social and economic philosophy to *connect* virtue and commerce (or ethics and economics) … (libertarians) are also required to demonstrate that commerce itself does not violate morality. It is not enough, therefore, to demonstrate the superiority of the liberal market order over its rivals in terms of efficiency, for libertarians have to show that this is consistent with a morality of freedom which reason commends to men.

Op. cit., p.7

… it might be helpful to refer briefly to the writings of Bernard Mandeville. In his justly famed Fable of the Bees he first proposed the aforementioned dichotomy between 'virtue' and 'commerce', a dichotomy which has haunted liberalism ever since. Mandeville maintained that the traditional and conventional axioms of morality were incompatible with those natural impulses of egoism and vice which promoted commercial well-being.

… the dominant tradition of western morality, that is, the tradition that defines moral conduct in terms of the suppression of natural, selfish impulses in the interests of abstractions such as 'society' or 'humanity'.

Op. cit., p.16

At first reading, the point that Barry is making appears to be essentially correct and that there is a serious dichotomy between the physical and the spiritual kingdoms. On closer inspection, however, Barry's argument is based on some fundamental misconceptions of the Judeo-Christian tradition; and a lack of understanding of Henry George.

1   Firstly, it is not true to say that the selfish impulses of individuals are required to be *suppressed*. They are, however, required to be *tempered*, and this is a very different thing. The Judeo-Christian tradition is concerned about the individual and his character, and this does not call for any subservience to abstractions such as 'society' or 'humanity' (Subservience to God, yes, but not to any human construct. Daniel was saved by the angels from becoming dinner after being thrown in the Lion's den because he would *not* bow to the statue of the king). *'Love thy neighbour (individual) as thyself'* is the command. And if one does not love oneself one cannot love the neighbour. Tempering of the character is like tempering of steel, it does not destroy or damage either steel, character or individual, it makes them stronger and better. In fact, Jesus said that he had come to give *'life in all its fullness'* John

10:10, and he clearly enjoyed a good party. Now that does not sound like the kind of message or example that Barry is talking about.

2   Secondly, if individuals are to be able to give to others, they must first have gained the means to do so. And as we have already seen there are only two ways of gaining the means, one is work, the other is robbery. The Bible is very clear here: '*Six days shalt thou labour ...*' – the work ethic is clearly and unequivocally encouraged. '*Thou shalt not steal*' – no ill-gotten gains allowed: respect the property of others. It would be hard to imagine greater endorsement of the commercial order than these commands. Biblical morality then is quite the reverse of conflicting with commercial life; it is actually a thoroughgoing amen to the productive process. Furthermore it is easy to find phrases like '*deal fairly with one another*', '*use honest weights and measures*', phrases that implicitly support trade and commerce.

3   Thirdly, Mandeville's argument simply falls to pieces in the light of the Oppenheimer/George analysis, on which Barry is silent. Mandeville says that it is the indolence, extravagance and luxury of the ruling class which provides work for the humble artisan. If the ruling class were to conform to Western morality – so the argument goes – the artisans would starve. This obviously ignores the Oppenheimer/George case, which says that freedom from oppressive taxation would more than outweigh any reduction in 'demand' from the ruling class. In fact, the Oppenheimer/George analysis explicitly states that commercial life would improve to a never before experienced level.

The existence of a *ruling* class is actually predicated on wholesale theft from a *subject* class. So the implementation of the Georgist solution, by abolishing political robbery, would conform the social order to the Law '*Thou shalt not steal*'. Here, our Minimal State *requires* the 'western morality' that Barry asserts is contradictory to it!

There is one sense in which Barry is, however, correct in his assertion. The *Established* Christian Church has, for many years, championed the welfare of the dispossessed through forcible appropriation from the producers by the State. The Established Church *appears* to be saying that commerce and virtue are essentially separate. However, just as Barry's examination of Classical Liberalism and Libertarianism concluded that it is more than one monolithic block, so we need to see that there is more than one version of 'Western Morality'. The Established Church does not, in this instance, represent the teachings of its founder. From the time that the Christian Church became the official religion of the Roman Empire, the message that the world received from the Established Church concerning matters of State have been persistently biased. And by its nature, the Established Church has the greatest political clout of all the branches of Christianity.

To those who take the trouble to read it in one of its modern translations, the Bible is clearly an appeal to the individual, and not to any form of social agglomeration. The message of Jesus was for individuals about individuals: to love God and one's neighbours. By contrast, the Established Church that calls with siren voice to the State to do what Jesus called individuals to do, is in fact way out of line with His teaching. So far out of line has it become in its active promotion of the 'welfare' State that it now works against the welfare of individuals.

The Social Gospel of Jesus can be summed up in his second commandment 'Love your neighbour as yourself'. This clearly means that we must treat each other as equals, or to put it in other words, all men have equal rights. This is where we get the ringing words of the U.S. Declaration of Independence: 'We hold these truths to be self-evident, that all men are created equal; that they are endowed by their Creator with certain unalienable rights ...'. Powerful words.

This Social Gospel does not mean Statism, socialism or any other State sponsored levelling, it simply means that you are responsible to take care of those around you as and when required. If Jesus had wanted it, I am sure that he could have said 'Go and lobby Caesar to raise taxation to give to the poor and needy'. No, instead he said 'Love your neighbour'. The responsibility rests with each one of us, the State has nothing to do with this. In fact some of his harshest words were reserved for power elites. King Herod he called a fox, but the religious leaders – the scribes and Pharisees – came in for the most withering condemnation. Seven times Jesus repeats the words 'Woe unto you scribes and Pharisees, hypocrites'. May the religious leaders of today not fall into such error! Jesus appeals to each individual to help others from their *own* resources, not from the resources of third parties: that would be both theft as well as hypocrisy.

Land rights

In fact the Bible is an absolutely unique source of values essential to the Libertarian order. We have already seen there is *'Six days shalt thou labour'*, and *'Thou shalt not steal'*. Furthermore we have the treatment of Land as a different order from other property.

> So when you sell land to your fellow Israelite or buy land from him, do not deal unfairly. The price is to be fixed according to the number of years the land can produce crops before the next year of Restoration. If there are many years, the price shall be higher, but if there are only a few years, the price shall be lower, because what is being sold is the number of crops the land can produce.
> Your land must not be sold on a permanent basis, because you do not own it; it belongs to God, and you are like foreigners who are allowed to make use of it.
> Leviticus, Chapter 25, v.14-16 & 23

Land was always the great promise for the Israelis: 'The Promised Land'. It was to be restored to its tribal ownership every fifty years, ruling out the possibility of creating a landless class. Once in every individual's adult life the Land was to be returned to all the people and not just left to the more 'successful' who had happened to appropriate more of it. Psalm 115, v.16, says: *'The heaven, even the heavens are the Lord's; but the Earth he has given to the children of men'.* The prophet Isaiah in Chapter 5, v. 8 excoriates the Land speculators, *'Woe to you who add house to house and join field to field till no space is left and you live alone in the land.'* Nehemiah, in Chapter 5, blows a gasket at the ruling elite who are extorting Land from the peasants in exchange for loans and assistance. He states that this is *'very evil'* (v.9), he also credits himself for not acquiring Land, in a prayer to God. Here there is clear Scriptural support for the equal rights of all in Land and therefore support for the Georgist Single Tax.

The Single Tax

On taxation itself, the most famous and influential words have been *'Render unto Caesar ...'* and they have been trotted out *ad nauseam* to justify taxation ever since. The context, however, was a trap question concerning the conflict between Roman and Hebrew laws, and it is likely that the answer was meant as a way out of the trap and was certainly not intended as the final and authoritative word on the subject, as it has in fact been treated.

Another incident which happened immediately prior to this event in Capernaum is rarely referred to or quoted but it would appear to be the real message about taxation that Jesus would give us. It is only recorded in the gospel of Matthew who had been a tax collector himself and is therefore likely to have paid particular attention to this incident. This story began when Peter was confronted in the streets of Capernaum by the Temple tax authorities (Matthew 17: 24-27). And Peter, being Peter, bluffed his way out of it saying that Jesus and he paid the tax. But when Peter got back to the place where they were staying, '*Jesus spoke up first*', demonstrating that he already knew what had gone on.

> Who pays duties or taxes to the kings of this world? The citizens or the foreigners?

When the disciple answered: '*The foreigners,*' Jesus replied:

> Well, then the citizens are free! However, we don't want to offend them, so go down to the lake and throw in a line. Open the mouth of the first fish you catch, and you will find a coin. Take the coin and pay the tax for both of us.

These words have a far greater significance than '*Render unto Caesar ...*' as they are spoken to and amongst friends, and at all times the conversation was under Jesus' complete control. And they have some very astonishing implications: – taxation is a means of oppression and it is not moral duty that compels us to pay, but expediency.

When he sent Peter to the lake to catch the fish with the coin in its mouth that was exactly enough to pay for their taxes, Jesus was working a miracle to show authority for his words: '*Well, then that means that the citizens don't have to pay. But we don't want to offend these people.*' Strangely this miracle is Jesus' only one that is not recorded as having happened – it is left as a command. I suggest that it remains a command for his followers today.

Peter was, after all, a fisherman by trade so Jesus sent him to do nothing more than go about his business, and after paying the tax, Peter would still be left with the full product of his Labour. And this is precisely the point Georgists make when they say that the Single Tax is not a tax but a commercial rent – the entrepreneur keeps 100% of what he produces. As we have seen above from Jesus' seven woes on the religious leaders, he was not afraid of giving offence where necessary, so we may wonder why not here? I suggest that it is simply a case of timing. When the time is right to offend these people, they shall be offended.

Free judicial service

The Biblical story of the exodus of Hebrew slaves from Egyptian oppression, and the foundling Israeli State in the Promised Land is intriguing. Moses was not only the mouthpiece of God, he also practised as the chief judge with an order of lesser judges under him. Apparently justice administered by this system was without charge. In the newly founded State, the head of State was the senior judge (presumably with lesser judges under them) and again this was a free service (see the book of Judges). This system lasted for three hundred years before the people asked Samuel, who was the last such judge/ruler to give them a king – something God was particularly displeased about (I Samuel, Chapter 8). So even though we cannot find a proposal for a free judicial service prior to Herbert Spencer, we here find one actually in practice thousands of years ago. It appears to have been practiced successfully for hundreds of years, and is an example for us today.

Individual rights

The Bible is a full and original source of individual rights, which, as Barry and Nozick both note, provide the *only* firm foundation for the libertarian political and economic philosophy. Indeed there is no comparable source for these rights in all philosophy in the whole world. This is why we find 'western morality' or Judeo/Christian culture directly or indirectly at the source of almost all impulses toward individual freedom. The Reformation, The Declaration of Independence, The Constitution of the U.S.A., abolition of slavery, women's rights, etc.

The prophet Malachi (Chapter 4, v. 2) wrote that we *'shall be as free and as happy as calves let out of a stall.'* To those who have witnessed such a scene, there is no more playful, energetic gambolling, expressive of the immanent joy of sheer living. Only such living poetry can give us a picture of the result of a State pattern that leaves the maximum amount of freedom and power in the hands of the individual: such is the dream of this book. We all want different things, so the State that leaves the individual free to choose what he wants (subject to not limiting anyone else's freedom) is the highest form of State.

The three proposals of this book, the Single Tax, the Minimal State and the Free Judicial Service all have clear Biblical sanction. We have looked at a few examples of these but I imagine that this topic has the potential for another whole book.

*

We began this chapter with Barry's concern that the capitalist, libertarian order may be at odds with 'western morality'. A little digging, however, makes clear that this is not remotely an issue, and in fact the reverse is the case. 'Western morality', Judeo-Christian tradition or the Bible – call it what you will – clearly authorises the political libertarianism and the Judicial State that is the subject of this book. Sadly the vast majority of the recipients of this tradition have not themselves come to this conclusion – many even champion and revere the State to the point of worshipping it. Furthermore, current State laws which tax Labour while allowing the earth's resources to fall into monopoly hands are diametrically opposed to Biblical authority. It therefore appears that there is a requirement for even more 'western morality' to infuse society before the oppressive State can be done away with. It looks like the Judeo-Christian tradition must increase before enough people see the State for the deceiving monster that it is.

The issue can be pressed even further. It appears that there is a significant *symbiotic* relationship between political libertarianism and biblical faith. In *Beyond Good Intentions* (1988 Crossway Books, p. 81) Doug Bandow writes:

> Rushdoony makes the intriguing observation that political and economic freedom – particularly independence from the paternal welfare state – has a spiritual dimension, since it forces men to walk by faith. 'Ultimately,' he writes, 'our faith must be in Christ or in Caesar, and it is better by far to walk by faith in Christ than to walk by sight under Caesar'. Certainly the wider the latitude of action allowed an individual the greater the variety of situations in which he must exercise moral judgement and seek to advance biblical principles; freedom also enhances his opportunity to enjoy God's creation.

So it would appear that not only is the political libertarianism of this book buttressed by 'western morality', but that that faith will, in turn, be bolstered by the political system proposed here. An ironic conclusion indeed!

Herbert Spencer points out in *Social Statics*, that an individual must control himself from within, or be controlled from without – there is no other way. Jesus expressly stated that the Kingdom was within each person. Therefore as individuals grow in self-control (the battleground of moral teaching), so the need for an active State diminishes, and the original motivations of State formation die away. Thus the greatest impetus to the achievement of the Minimal State lies in the advancement of the personal morality which was fulfilled by Jesus. If the Church, through her preaching and teaching, will raise up men and women who will accept responsibility for their lives and the lives of their loved ones, there would be no demand for a paternalistic 'Welfare State'.

Franz Oppenheimer, in ending his essay *The State* and pointing to the potential for the future, makes the analogy of the history of man and the State, with the Crucifixion of Christ and his resurrection:

> This has been the path of suffering and of salvation of humanity, its Golgotha and its resurrection into an eternal kingdom – from war to peace, from the hostile splitting up of the hordes to the peaceful unity of mankind, from brutality to humanity, from the exploiting State of robbery to the Freemen's Citizenship.

Human history is the crucifixion of man – the resurrection is ahead.

*

All things that are part of nature must be subject to natural Law. When the State follows the Law laid down for it in nature, human society will discover the Laws that govern its own existence, and will conform to them simply because – in the end – man's free will and the will of the creator are one and the same thing. When man is in tune with God the blessed state is reached. Here we may find the answer to the conundrum posed by that old story of our original ancestors being thrown out of the garden of paradise because of their *disobedience*. When we follow natural Law we will again be *obeying* our Creator and we may expect the condition of paradise to return.

CHAPTER 10

Wither the State!

*'The great difference between the real statesman and the pretender
is that ... the one acts on enduring principles, the other
acts on expedience.'*
Edmund Burke

*'Those who want to do everything all at once,
end up doing nothing at all.'*
Samuel Johnson

T HE PROMISE that under communism the State would 'wither away'
was either a grotesque joke or a grandiose delusion. Either way, Karl
Marx could not have been further from the truth, as the State has achieved
some of its worst excesses in the guise of the communist fallacy. Not only
have the freedoms of those living under its cruel regime been brought to
naught but many millions of its own citizens have been killed in the
process. Nietzsche's description of the State as the 'coldest of all cold
monsters' comes closest to revealing the State's true nature. The Conflict
Theory of its origin shows that this monster was birthed in greed, violence
and bloodshed and that it exists today only by sucking power from the
citizens it pretends to protect. *'Who is like the beast and who can make war
against him?'* (Revelations, 13, v. 4).

The Minimal State of Frederick Bastiat is the smallest proposed State in
all political philosophy. It has no function other than the defence of its
citizens. This is as close as we can get to the State withered away; but it
will never get there on its own, withering away like a leaf dying at the
end of its useful life. It will have to *be* withered away, or to continue

the imagery from Revelation, the dragon will have to be tied up and thrown in the lake of burning sulphur. A major effort will be required to see the State's functions pruned back to its bare necessities; and this is the topic of this chapter. Effort maybe, but the victory is assured: '*He will persist until He causes Justice to triumph.*'

There can be few direct cutbacks in State meddling until its foot is first removed from the necks of citizens and we are allowed to produce and trade freely; that is without taxation. The first step, then, towards the State of Freedom and Justice that we seek is to remove all taxes from Labour and the product of Labour, and at the same time replace them with the natural resource rent. In 1988 I wrote a paper titled 'Budget for Tax Abolition Ireland' which can be found in Appendix D at the end of this book. In the paper I examine the rate and order of abolition of all the various taxes levied by all forms of government in Ireland. The arguments remain exactly the same years later, though there have been some changes to the proportion of the various taxes. Principally VAT has grown to become first equal with income taxes in size.

The order for abolition and the argument in full can be read in the appendix but I will summarise the proposal here. First to go must be those taxes whose removal will clear the way for the implementation of the alternative revenue source. These include all direct taxes on properties as well as those on their purchase and sale, such as Stamp Duties, VAT, and Capital Gains etc. The second priority are the those taxes whose contribution to the exchequer is so small that to remove them completely would do little to the overall revenue total, but would give considerable administrative and compliance relief. Any taxes that collect less than 0.25% of State revenue would fall into this category. In 1988 these included Table waters excise, Cheques and Bills stamp duties, Agricultural levies, Stocks and shares stamp duties, foreign travel excise, Video excise, Mechanical lighters and Matches excise. Today the names and details may have changed but the stupidity has not.

This leaves the two major imposts, income taxes and VAT, along with a number of lesser line items such as corporation profits tax, excise on cars and parts, motor vehicle licences, insurance and bank levies. Income taxes are direct taxes on Labour and therefore more pernicious than VAT, so should be removed first. We can group all forms of levies, taxes and charges on income under the one heading since it does not matter what names they are given, their disincentive effects are all the same. This gives us the opportunity to remove them in the most employment benefiting manner possible, to progressively raise the zero tax threshold for all the various charges simultaneously. This will free those on lowest incomes first while at the same time giving some relief to those on higher income levels. Given a five year term of government the budget looked as follows.

Budget for Tax Abolition, Ireland 1988

		£m
Budget 1	Capital Gains Tax gone	13
	Capital Acquisitions Tax gone	25
	Stamp Duties on property gone	59
	Residential Property Tax gone	2
	Rates gone	170
	All taxes less than 0.25% of revenue gone	70
	Income Tax reduction (17%)	661
		1,000
Budget 2	Income Tax reduction (31%)	1,200
Budget 3	Income Tax reduction (35%)	1,400
Budget 4	Income Tax abolished (17%)	654
	Non-road fuel excises gone	58
	Insurance and bank levies gone	85
	Customs gone.	88
	Vehicle licences gone.	139
	Excises on cars and parts, gone	140
	Corporations Profits Tax gone	257
		1,421
Budget 5	Abolish VAT	1,585

Up to date figures would bring a few changes to this picture: first, that the overall numbers would be much bigger. Secondly, now that VAT raises just as much as Income taxes, it would take the last three budgets to abolish VAT, while it would take the first three to abolish income taxes; Budget 3 would be split between finishing off Income tax and starting to reduce VAT. Finally the names on the smaller revenue lines may be different. Overall the picture is remarkably similar today, and – with similar variations – the same picture is likely to emerge in other States around the world.

The only new question today is how to abolish VAT in three years? Should it be done by reducing the VAT Rates or abolishing some of them, or by removing VAT from selected trades? Or even a combination of the above? Once the political will is there, I am sure that these questions will find easy answers. They are not the most profound, and do not have to be answered here. What is important is to envision the State being pruned back; its oppressive arm being lopped off. This is just the beginning.

During this period of removing taxation, the Land Value Tax can be introduced, and then the rate increased with each budget to replace *most* of the revenue lost through the tax abolition process. I say 'most' because it is immediately possible to withdraw the State functions that attempt to stimulate employment and business. The effect of removing taxes on Labour and its products will have a much bigger stimulus effects on employment and trade than all other dedicated government efforts. From the start, all government's effort to increase (in any way) business, enterprise, capitalisation, economic modernisation – or whatever else it may be touted as – can be completely removed. The banking system and money supply can be reformed by removing legal tender laws which will allow private money and banking enterprises to start up. The immediate effect of the new 'Single Tax' regime will be to ensure full employment and steady economic growth. The economy will start to suck in Labour and Capital from abroad and wages will be pushed up as landowners compete for Labour. Now the scene is set for the real pruning of the State to begin. The big three, health, education and welfare can now be carefully and sensitively removed from the State grip.

Professor Barry at the conclusion of *On Classical Liberalism and Libertarianism* becomes depressed at the prospect of the impossibility of dismantling the State due to the vested interests involved, especially those of the civil servants who form a vast voting block. The thought is that this section of society is so large that its vote will prevent the election of leaders who will implement the Minimal State. But this line of thinking fails to take into account the Georgist solution that will radically remake the private sector of the economy in such a way that will attract State employees away from their sinecures. An economy that is growing strongly, securely and is well balanced, sucking in Labour and Capital from surrounding nations, will find well paid and secure employment for any State employees made redundant or who go voluntarily. The Georgist solution changes the dynamic and makes way for chainsaw pruning of the State to occur.

A thriving and permanently stable economy allows for the complete removal of most State welfare services simply because free people trading to their heart's content will secure the welfare of all without effort. This is the beauty of the 'invisible hand'. Welfare can swiftly be trimmed to a midway point where it is a minimal safety net; and even this can be done away with after a certain period of time. This time allows the voluntary sector to come back into play. Likewise, education will take care of itself so long as there are always well paid and secure jobs in the general economy for those looking for them, and this *will* be the case in the Georgist economy. As we have described above, education will be a lifelong pursuit, matching means to ends. We might divide education into primary, secondary and tertiary level, so the State can be removed from the latter first, then secondary and finally primary. Removing the State from all involvement in health will be tricky due to the life and death issues potentially involved. A simple way to do it may be that the State privatises all services at once but gives citizens health credits inversely based on income levels, and then either the credits are progressively reduced to disappear after, say, twenty years or the income thresholds are decreased in a similar manner.

The biggest problem with removing so much State function over say twenty years is not so much with the techniques of how to do it but with the social dislocation involved, and that people will have to think for themselves in areas where they do not currently have any choices. We may be talking of up to 40% of all State jobs changing to private sector, and this is what concerns Barry. But in fact the issue is not so difficult. Most of those affected will simply wake up one morning to find that their boss is no longer a bureaucrat but a businessman. They may have exactly the same job or function but a different working environment. They may even find they are effectively working for themselves, subcontracted to hospitals or schools or other services; or actually shareholders of the organisation for which they work. Retraining may not even be necessary but a different mindset will be required, a different attitude. In the private sector the customer is king because the customer pays the bills and ultimately the wages. This is not true for the public sector, where the customer is just a cog in the wheel, and a little one at that. This is much of the reason to make these changes in the first place and one of its major benefits. Finally, the patient, the student, the worker is the one who calls the shots: the customer – who is all of us – is king.

Once the radical surgery has been performed on the State and its wild, extravagant growths removed, there is one final requirement to reach the dream of this book. The justice system must be overhauled in such a way that there are no charges placed on anyone seeking justice and their day in court. The process of moving towards this end would begin immediately following the abolition of taxation. There is so much injustice (not giving what is due) involved in the system of current taxation that it makes no sense for one arm of the State to be involved in a major theft operation while the other arm is trying to adjudicate such. Only when the major theft operation has ceased can the State sensibly begin to provide true justice. Perhaps this may be done by the State providing public defenders for all from an otherwise private sector legal system. Or should the State 'nationalise' the whole legal system? Past experience of the State taking over a whole sector should make us say that the first idea is better. Again I am sure that when push comes to shove and the political will exists to provide a free judicial service, a way will be found. We do not need to provide the full details here.

The State will not *'wither away'* of its own accord; the enormous structural surgery required to make the monster humane will take vision, planning, commitment and execution. I hope I have given some vision and sketched a few plans. Now it requires popularisation and the political will large enough to have a government voted in to implement the laws required to make it happen. This is the basis of a State conformable with the Laws of nature; and a good case could then be made that the law which instituted such a regime would then be both statute and natural Law.

The Freedom and Justice party

No nation or State in the world today comes close to the State represented in this book. Even the freest nations today are far from the ideal State of Freedom and Justice. The U.S.A., the unchallenged leader of the free world, has gone a long way down the road in the *opposite* direction and even seems to be gaining speed along the way. However, there is no other nation that so self-consciously holds the torch of freedom aloft for all to see. Lady Liberty is not just a statue but a reality that lives in the hearts of many Americans, and I find it difficult to imagine that her people will not again come to their senses and begin the march back to *'the home of the brave and the land of the free'*.

Or maybe it will be Ireland, or Israel, or the Czech Republic, or Taiwan or Thailand. Somewhere that the people love freedom and want to see it brought to completion by combining it with justice; and who are willing to fight to achieve it. Or will it be some backward African State that is currently being run as the private fiefdom of a tribal chief? If that chief saw the light, he would not have to dismantle a large welfare State apparatus, just change the revenue source and remove corruption from his administration. However it happens, one day, somewhere, it will happen, and the world will watch with awe as Labour and Capital flock to a nation populated by a prosperous and peaceful people. Quickly a domino effect will occur as neighbouring nations rush to catch up on the road to Freedom and Justice.

In much of the democratic world, election time is greeted with a yawn. Most political parties offer a similar recipe of half-baked ideas that have sickened the appetites of the electorate for years. Politicians promise much (that the State will do much) and deliver little or nothing. None of them really get the problem or the solution. All they offer is 'More of the State!', 'Multinational Government', 'Global Government!'. Meanwhile the citizens feel more and more remote and stay at home on election day.

The State of Freedom and Justice is so radically different from anything on offer to the freedom lover that it is unlikely to be endorsed or campaigned for by any existing party. So to effect the change, we may need to form our own party. I propose The Freedom and Justice Party with the slogans 'Power to the People!' and 'Down with State government, up with self-government!'

Speed of change

Those who agree wholeheartedly with any or all the reforms of this book often want them to be implemented immediately. I too wish, but these reforms are likely to take place gradually as the perception of their need grows – however much the libertarian Georgist might like to see the transformation carried out straight away. Gradualism takes into account practical realities; as William Lloyd Garrison, the abolitionist stated:

> Urge immediate abolition as earnestly as we may, it will, alas! be gradual
> abolition in the end. We have never said that slavery would be overthrown
> by a single blow; that it ought to be, we shall always contend.

The same can be said of taxation and State power today. It is therefore up to all those in positions of power who have the interests of society at heart to make progress whenever opportunities present themselves, and to avoid any steps which lead in the opposite direction.

For the apparatus of the State, the implications of this thesis are both straightforward and comparatively easy to implement. The challenge is likely to be for society – composed of free individuals – voluntarily to organise those functions that will be shed by the State. Particularly this will mean that those associations which organised health, welfare and education, will need to be revitalised. This calls for a great restoration and recommitment of faith groups particularly, and all other voluntary groups, to care for the sick or to supply whatever needs become apparent to them.

This revitalisation of faith groups must be paralleled or preceded by effective preaching of the Kingdom within, including the denouncement of Stateolatory. Only when the worship of the State is removed from the hearts and minds of a sufficient number of individuals, will the Judicial State be instituted. For when people turn to the State and its laws to enforce the will of God, they turn away from the power of God. They set up human laws and institutions higher than God; they worship the State. To make human laws against immoral (but non-invasive) behaviour is to say that God is incapable of transforming people; it is to turn to a false god.

Know your enemies

The monstrous State has been around since the dawn of civilization and it will not go easily. It will require a major battle on the part of lovers of freedom and justice everywhere to see it cut back to its necessary functions. When doing battle, it is well to know who the enemy is, what he looks like and how he is armed. So let us take a look.

Doubt and depression. Belief and hope are the antidotes to these two enemies. As I have written earlier, we need to *believe* that there is an order written into nature – natural Law – and that it exists for government and the State just as much as it exists for human psychology and the motion of the planets. We need to have this faith and hold it close at all times so that we will not be assailed by doubt. This faith will breed *hope*. Hope is looking forward to something that does not exist yet, but we can work in eager anticipation toward the goal, given this hope.

Infantile regression is allied to Doubt and Depression. A few years ago a pop song hit the charts in which the singer, caught in the act of infidelity, repeats the refrain *'"Twasn't me!'* as he rehearses all the things he should have done to make sure he wasn't caught. This refrain has become for a new generation a conscious expression of denial of responsibility; but they are only expressing the grown-up world they see around them. The spectacle of mature, and otherwise responsible, adults looking to offload responsibility for their family's education, health and welfare seems to me to be a form of infantile regression. '"Twasn't me – Can't be me!' This infantile regression is both cause and effect of State welfarism. The more that people surrender responsibility to the State, the more incapable they become in stepping up to the plate and accepting the responsibility that nature puts upon them, and so they increase the excuses for the State to take over.

Land speculators. The only business that will disappear under the Georgist solution will be that of Land speculation. It was the likes of Cornell who owned much of western America, who founded the profession of Neo-classical Economics through his university, deliberately undermining Classical Economics – of which Henry George and his book, *Progress and Poverty* was the flower.[14] Today the Land speculator is connected with many politicians like ivy round trees – and ivy makes the tree grow crooked. Tree and ivy are very difficult to separate and constitute one of the major reasons politicians have not gotten the Georgist message before now. In Ireland, the judicial enquiries into the connections between politicians in high office and brown envelopes stuffed with cash donated by Land speculators has been an ongoing saga for many years. It will have no end till the Georgist solution is enacted.

Land speculation, in the eyes of many, is an honourable and legitimate business if bribes are kept out of it. But it is not so. Few today would say that slave ownership was an honourable and legitimate business – far from it. But the two are not far apart. The story of Robinson Crusoe and his slave, Man Friday is a classic and makes our point. On a limited

---

[14] See Mason Gaffney and Fred Harrison, *The Corruption of Economics*, Shepheard-Walwyn, 1994, for a full account of this story.

plot of Land, it makes no difference if Crusoe owns Friday or the Land! The effect is precisely the same. Crusoe gets all his work done by Friday and has not only the weekend off but the week as well. Friday is either slave or serf but still has to do the work for both of them. Land speculators are the moral equivalent of slave owners. We can do without them.

Unconscious Land speculators are another enemy we need to be aware of. Many people seem to feel that there is nothing wrong with the idea of property prices escalating in such a way that their wealth increases without effort on their part. There has been much talk over the years of a property ladder and that the problem is for first time owners to get a foot on the first rung of the ladder. The true metaphor and problem are a little different. A more accurate analogy is really that of a property escalator, one onto which the property owner steps to be slowly but steadily raised to dizzying heights. This dizziness prevents clear thinking on the issue. In reality the elevation is in the price of Land and it comes at the expense of wages and returns to Capital. The un-propertied therefore have to save up from their now scrimped income to afford the first step on the property escalator which gets progressively further from their reach as the boom period reaches its climax, when, suddenly, the escalator grinds to a halt and actually goes into reverse, throwing those on the bottom steps off.

Again this whole problem dissolves when Labour receives its full reward and there are no taxes levied on those rewards, and also when Land ownership is legitimised by payment of a market determined rent. The unconscious Land speculator is much more common than the conscious speculator: he is most property owners whether we like it or not. We may be him whether we like it or not. The important issue is to see how it affects our thinking and to not let ourselves be dizzied by the process. If you were a shareholder in a company that owns slaves you would bail out as soon as you found out the truth. The only way to bail out from the similar moral problem of being a landowner is to work towards the Georgist solution.

Ignorance. Lack of knowledge of any problem is a problem in itself, but once one gains understanding one has the opportunity to deal with the real issue. Here we come across the many genuine and sincere people on both left and right who work hard trying to make a better world. The left tend to appeal to the State to do more while the right try to reduce the

State's powers but neither get to the real issues because they do not understand them. The left ought to work towards the common right of all to Land, they should get fully behind the Georgist cause, and maybe when they see the issues clearly they will do so. The right tend to see that the State is much of the problem and that taxation destroys incentives. When they see this with complete clarity, they can work towards the complete *abolition* of taxes rather than just tax *reduction*. Furthermore they should work towards the Minimal State for that is their gut instinct. The politically active should be our best allies once they have the knowledge, they are enemies now only because they are ignorant.

The vast majority of the voting population are genuine hard working people who try daily to do the right thing. The only thing that stops them from voting in politicians who will institute the reforms of this book is that they do not know what the right thing is in the field of political philosophy. When they know and understand they will do what is right.

The sympathetic critic. Perhaps the saddest enemy of this idea is the one who understands and is sympathetic towards it but who deems it 'idealistic'. This accusation is doubly wounding. The first problem is that it is an accusation by *implication*: it implies that the idea cannot be practised, that *it can exist in the form of an idea only.* But the accuser does not say this directly so he cannot be rebutted.

Secondly, this accusation is not only false but it is true in reverse. Not only is the idea entirely practical – because, as we have seen, it conforms with natural Law – but it is the opposing ideas which are themselves impractical (read 'idealistic'). Human pride continues to disregard the will of the Creator and His natural Laws, attempting to establish puny human constructs such as communism, socialism, welfare-statism, etc., trying to put them into practice by force. These always and everywhere end in failure as they come up against natural Laws, and they fail at terrible human cost.

In the end, however, the truth will win out and Justice will triumph! The only question is: Will you be part of it?

The Story of the Book

I NEVER INTENDED writing a book. My first efforts at setting down
some ideas on politics began as a few photocopied pages titled 'Labour
Taxation' which I shared among a few friends. It appeared quite insane
to me that in those days of massive unemployment in Ireland, the largest
single revenue source was taxes on wages/earnings/employment. Mum
observed my efforts and predicted that one day I would write a book and,
to this end, her last gift to me was the 1978 *Encyclopaedia Britannica*.

The earliest impetus for this book probably dates back to ten years
before I was born when my grandfather's family's cotton mill, 'Swadeshi',
was threatened with nationalization by the incoming independent Indian
government of 1947. This forced the sale of the enterprise to the native
Indian wholesaler who had made his fortune alongside that of Swadeshi.
My grandfather was a Yorkshireman whose home was in Essex to where
he hoped to retire, but the British government at that time had an
eye-watering, gut-wrenching top tax rate of 97.5%[15] on Capital, and
Yorkshiremen do not like giving away their hard earned 'brass' that easily!
At that time, Ireland was a Capital Tax haven so granddad purchased a
property in Rathdrum, Co. Wicklow where he came to reside. I did not
know granddad personally but I picked up on the depth of a tax exile's
emotion from my Dad. *'Iniquitous!'* was a deeply felt, highly stressed and
oft repeated word my father used to describe any tax that would deny the
individual of his hard earned money. I understood the sentiment but also
understood that government must raise revenue somehow. The arrow
was stretched in the string and the bow bent for release.

---

[15] 'Nineteen shillings and sixpence in the Pound,' as my father's wrinkled cousin, Richard, put it!

As a teenager in the mid 1970s I was an active environmentalist and I wrote letters to the Prime Ministers of Russia and Japan as part of the Friends of the Earth anti-whaling campaign. In 1981 my Dad asked me to take on the management of the family farm which had been home for all my twenty-four years. Suddenly my environmental leanings were challenged by the need of the farm to make a living for all concerned: Chemical v Organic? Living, growing hedges v sterile electric fencing? Chemical weed-killers v hand rogueing of weeds? These became the questions that now taxed my mathematical and logically inclined mind. State theft of hard earned brass, high unemployment, and running a commercial farm as a committed environmentalist now combined to make me realise that taxes on Labour (earning a modest living) were utterly wrong and unjustifiable, and had to be abolished. But how should the State fund itself? The arrow had left the bow.

I took a week long break from the farm and locked myself away in the highest cottage on Slieve Na Mon, Co. Tipperary with my *Encyclopedia Britannica*. I researched all the various types of tax that I could find, with one burning question. What did each tax incentivize or disincentivise and was the incentive effect negative or positive? The only 'tax' that appeared to have any positive effects was, what was then called 'Rates' (a form of property tax). Inasmuch as it was a tax on buildings or improvements it had negative effects, *but*, inasmuch as it was a tax on the site or Land it had positive economic effects. In this it stood alone. The cross references in the *Encyclopedia* lead to Site Value Tax and to Henry George. Quickly it dawned on me that the abolition of taxation on Labour (with its replacement by the Site Value Tax) would have a far greater effect towards environmental improvement than all the dedicated legislation ever could or would. I dropped my environmentalism and joined the then startup Green Party, which had some members who understood the Land Value Tax to some degree. I also joined the International Georgist organizations who met regularly and who kept Henry George's books and ideas alive. I wrote and self-published (1984) a 12-page booklet called Raising Revenue Without Taxation which has been expanded into Chapter 4 of this book.

The declining influence of the Georgist movement made me reassess my position. Not that there was any question about 'The Single Tax' being the correct revenue source for all government. I had worked it out for myself and now found that many others had come to the same conclusion, including Henry George; and there were a number of different starting points for this same conclusion. The question now formed in my mind: If the Single Tax were introduced, what effect would this have on the requirements for Government expenditure? And that question became: What are the proper functions of Government? This now became my pursuit. The arrow was in full flight.

Within the Georgist movement the full political spectrum is apparent, from those who wish to see the State give everyone a living wage, to anarchists (in the true, non-violent, sense of that word). It was in the London HQ of the International Union for Land Value Taxation and Free Trade (now the IU) where I found a copy of Frederick Bastiat's *The Law*. I did not, at first reading, realise what a piece of dynamite was enclosed within its slim volume. The concept of a State that only impinged on the individual if it (the State) was threatened from outside or if any of its citizens were threatened by another; this Minimal State took my breath away and I was simply unable to process what it meant. At much the same time, and from the same source, I found Frank McEachran's book *Freedom – the only end*. Only by reading and re-reading this book did I finally get my head around the Minimal State and could then see how it would work – and work so much better than the setups we have today. Having surrendered all the instinctive objections to the Minimal State, I realised it was deficient in one thing: Justice would have to be a free government service and not something money could buy. If it cost money – it appeared to me – it could not be Justice. That idea was confirmed when I found Herbert Spencer's letter. By 1992 all three main elements of the book were in place and I was ready to publish – or so I thought.

In the mid 1980s at a Georgist Conference in Cambridge, England I met Anthony Werner, a publisher with an appreciation of Georgist books. He had read my Raising Revenue Without Taxation and asked me if I had done any more writing as he was keen to get more Georgist work published. It was Anthony who first gave me the idea that my writing was more than an effort to straighten out my own head; it could actually become … a book! Since then he has been a continued source of encouragement as I have from time to time sent him updates of the manuscript. 'Shows promise but needs improvement' was the subliminal feedback I received. 1992, 2001, then 2009, I always got the same answer.

Over thirty years the working title has changed but I was never happy with any of them – *Principles of Statecraft, Justice to the Nations* among others. Only in 2009 did I get one that I felt as ease with, *The State of Freedom and Justice*, and another hurdle was crossed. The twenty plus years of delays in publishing were disguised blessings; two more important points had to surface.

In 2010 the office of the President of Ireland ran a competition for the best novel idea that would fundamentally transform the Irish economy. I felt I was in with a chance if I could condense thirty years writing into three pages. My entry went nowhere but the effort showed up a break in the chain of logic in my conjunction of George and Bastiat. I had read and reread it for twenty-five years and had not noticed the misstep every time. Immediately I rewrote it as it now stands.

In Ireland in September 2007 Land values, having been on a rocket ride upward for a number of years, peaked and came crashing down. Then in September 2008 the Irish Banking System collapsed. Here I saw, in 3D, vivid Technicolor and surround sound, the effect of a Land price crash on the banking system, and I was appalled by the lack of Georgist analysis by media, financial and political people alike. I looked for evidence of other occasions when the Land price crash had caused banking failures and did not take long to find Philip Anderson's book, *The Secret Life of Real Estate*, which documented a regularly repeating cycle of exactly the same phenomena that had occurred almost continuously since 1800. This confirmed my sense that the financial sector and banking industry should be among the strongest supporters of the 'Single Tax'. This seemed like serendipity times two: the Minimal State requires that money and banking be private enterprise, but financial stability requires the 'Single Tax'. Like a king piece in a jigsaw puzzle everything now came together. The arrow had hit its mark.

Writing did not come easily to me for the first forty-five years of my life for two reasons. The first was (and remains to some extent) a problem with my musculo-skeletal system. Writing could be discomforting or even painful. Writing essays in school was especially difficult, two-thirds the way down an A4 page and the writing would start to become illegible – even for me! This condition has required osteopathy and physiotherapy for most of my adult life, as well as the surgical removal of two discs from my spine.

More debilitating, however, was my shyness, part of which was a fear of expressing myself in written form. Aged eight I started boarding school where Sunday morning's only class was to write a letter home, and we were allowed to go out to play when we had submitted a satisfactory effort to the supervising teacher. I was always last out and my effort was invariably a copy of the bullet points the teacher had added to the

blackboard every fifteen minutes or so. Even aged ten, the week I got
news of the birth of my baby brother John, the weekend letter was the
same.

This barrier to expressing myself lead all my writing to be hesitant
and tentative, and goes a long way to explain why I preferred farming to
university. Many times when I had left this manuscript aside for a while
I would come back to read parts of it and wonder what it was I had been
trying to say. In 2007 I was finally delivered from this crippling unease.
The emotional switch happened on the carpet of a therapist's floor when
the raw pain of my father's abandoning me, aged 8, on my first day at
boarding school, the experience of loss, shame, guilt and rejection
suddenly became the most hilarious thing that had ever happened in my
life. From gut wrenching roaring crying to side-splitting, tear streaming,
infectious, contagious roaring laughter that swept up those present
and which stopped only when the pain in the tummy muscles became
unbearable!

Proof that the experience was real, deep and life changing came quickly;
the homework our therapist gave to be completed in two weeks' time was
to write out our childhood stories. I groaned inwardly at the assignment
and thought that if, in two weeks I could produce three A4 pages, I would
have done well. When I finally made myself sit down, the words, phrases,
sentences, paragraphs and pages came tumbling, gushing, streaming out.
A dam had broken, and when fifteen pages later I reviewed the result,
I realised I was witnessing a miracle. Gone were all the crossings out, the
infill arrows, the redistribution of thought arrows that normally graced
my pages like spiders fighting ink battles. I held fifteen pages of fluent
thought, emotion and story-telling such I had never seen in my life!

And the miracle was real. Some months later I resumed work on this
book after a long break. In the past I would be pleased if I could get a few
original paragraphs or sentences strung together in a whole day's work.
Now I sat down to do a badly needed rewrite of the Money and Banking
chapter. I amazed and delighted myself by completing the whole thing
in a couple of weekends. Truly a new world had opened up to me. I had
finally found the 'voice' for my writing for which I had been searching in
vain all the previous years. Since then I have rewritten almost the whole
book.

Professor Nozick, writing in the Preface to his book *Anarchy, State and
Utopia*, paints a vivid picture of the misgivings he felt about his book. He
likened the experience to physically shoving ideas in one side of a closely

packed enclosure, only to go around the other side to find the fence broken and ideas falling out which required pushing back in again, and so on. My experience of writing this book has been entirely opposite. For most of the years it has felt like I had picked up the end of a tiny piece of thread, hauling it in to find it become a piece of string, further hauling bringing in thicker and thicker rope till finally it became the strongest possible chain. Lately the analogy would be the piecing together of an enormous jigsaw puzzle which had been worked on by generations of the finest hearts and minds the world has seen, yet the picture is incomplete. The final realization, that a Free Banking system – required by the Minimal State – would itself require the Single Tax to work properly, is like the king piece in the jigsaw. The main elements are all now clearly visible and the whole picture holds together rigidly in its own strength. There may be a few areas of detail to infill but it is now only a matter of time before it can be said, *'It is finished!'*

APPENDIX A

The Five Men

IN THE COURSE of this book I introduce the work of five historical figures whose contributions to the world of ideas have largely been airbrushed from the halls of academia. For many readers, this book is likely the first time they have met these men, so a little resume of each is given below, in the order that they appear in the book.

Franz Oppenheimer was born in Berlin on 30th March 1864. His book *The State* (1908) presents the Conflict Theory of the Origin of the State. He died in Los Angeles on 30th September 1943.

Original in Central Zionist Archive, Jerusalem.

Frederic Bastiat was born in Bayonne, France in June 1801. His bestseller *The Law* (1850) gives us the natural Law which governs the State: the Law of Legitimate Force. He died in Rome on Christmas Eve 1850.

Henry George was born in Philadelphia, Pennsylvania in September 1839. His bestseller *Progress and Poverty* (1879) presents the case for The Single Tax on Land values to replace all taxes on Labour and Capital. He died during a run for mayor of New York in October 1897.

John Locke was born in Wrington, near Bristol in the summer of 1632. His book, *The Second Treatise on Civil Government* (1689), gives us the Law of Property rights. He died in England in October 1704.

Herbert Spenser was born in Derby, England, in April 1820. A prodigious author who promoted Land Value Taxation up to 1851, but then recanted. His Minimal State ideas were very similar to Frederic Bastiat's, but his 1843 letter proposing a Free Judicial Service is the reason he appears here. He died December 1903 in Brighton.

APPENDIX B

Two More Men

TWO OTHER men have been very influential in the writing of this book, but till 2002 both were very much alive. As a 'student' of both, I was shocked to learn of their untimely deaths, Nozick aged 63 in 2002 and Barry aged 64 in 2008. I had met Barry for a pub lunch once when I was passing through Buckingham in the early 1990s.

Robert Nozick (16th November 1938-23rd January 2002) was a Harvard professor of philosophy who did political philosophy for only four or five years and who otherwise made major contributions in epistemology, rational choice theory and the philosophy of mind and ethics.

His prizewinning book, *Anarchy, State and Utopia*, published in 1974 by Basic Books, was largely a rebuttal of the redistributive liberalism of his fellow Harvard philosopher and adversary John Rawls. But the book has become larger than the man; later in life Nozick renounced extreme libertarianism.

Norman P. Barry (25th June 1944-21st October 2008) was Professor of Social and Political Theory at the University of Buckingham, the only private university in Britain. Also he was a visiting scholar at Bowling Green State University in Ohio and at the Liberty Fund in Indianapolis, as well as being a member of the academic advisory council of the Institute of Economic Affairs.

An enthusiast for Frederic Bastiat and his book *The Law*, Norman published *On Classical Liberalism and Libertarianism* in 1987 with St. Martin's Press. (Perfect timing, Norman – thanks!)

APPENDIX C

Supporters of Henry George
or the Land Value Tax

Dr. Thomas Nulty, Bishop of Meath, *Back to the Land*, 1881.
   http://www.wealthandwant.com/docs/Nulty_BttL.html
Adam Smith, *The Wealth of Nations*, Methuen & Co., 1904 ed., Book V,
   Chapter II, Part II, 1st article, pp. 328-9.
John Stuart Mill, *Principles of Political Economy*, full edition, George
   Routledge, London, pp. 162-3.
Herbert Spencer, *Social Statics*, 1850 ed., Robert Schalkenback Foundation,
   New York.
The Physiocrats, see *Encyclopaedia Britannica*, 15th ed.
Thomas Jefferson, see *Encyclopaedia Britannica*, 15th ed.
Abraham Lincoln, Letter to William S. Wait, March 2nd 1839, from *The
   Political Thoughts of Abraham Lincoln*, edited by Current, 1967, Bobbs-
   Merrill Co. Inc.
Thomas Paine, *Rights of Man*, 1795, in *Paine's Works*.
Michael Davitt, see *Encyclopaedia Britannica*, 15th ed.
Winston Churchill, 'On Human Rights', speech in House of Commons,
   May 4th 1909.
Albert Einstein, letter to Mr. E.P. DuPont, December 13th 1935, Albert
   Einstein estate.
Leo Tolstoy, 'A Great Inequity', pp. 284-7, in *Recollections and Essays*,
   O.U.P. World's Classics Series. Also a consistent theme in the novel
   Resurrection.
Sun Yat Sen, *Fundamentals of National Reconstruction*.
Milton Friedman, report in *Human Events*, November 1978.

Budget for Tax Abolition
Ireland, May 1988

(Unpublished paper by Michael Horsman)

Introduction

THE PROPOSAL to abolish taxation rests on two assumptions: (i) that any and all taxes on Labour and the product of Labour, tend to discourage production, (ii) there is a perfectly feasible method of raising revenue without taxation, based on the idea most closely linked with America's economist and social reformer, Henry George (See George's *Progress and Poverty*, or the present author's 'Raising Revenue without Taxation').

This paper will primarily address the method and order for removing taxation. Some budget timetables will be given for illustration, they are tentative, however, because they will depend on the political will to implement the reform.

Aim

The aim of this proposal is to completely remove those taxes which fall on socially positive production (such as food, clothing and housing) in the most expedient manner. It does not address itself to (i) taxes on things commonly considered social evils, such as drink, tobacco, and betting, or (ii) levies which may be considered direct payment for services rendered, such as road fuel duties and local authority service charges, or (iii) licences of various sorts

This exclusivity may be excused on the grounds that to reform 81.5% of government revenue, equal to about 6.6 billion pounds, is sufficient for one project.

Nor will this paper discuss the introduction of the replacement revenue. It may be assumed that alternative revenue is raised on a one for one basis, but see end of paper for discussion of potential for a reduced government budget.

Why reform?

Almost every budget in modern history contains an element of schizophrenia: taxes on drink and tobacco are justified because these 'goods' are considered social evils (with the inference that taxes on them reduces production/consumption) while taxes on 'good' goods are justified by the exchequer requirement for revenue. This schizophrenia can only be integrated in the following way: (i) *All* taxation raises revenue, therefore it is illegitimate to use the revenue raising argument for any *particular* tax. (ii) *All* taxes discourage the object they are levied on, whether the object is 'good' or 'bad', so the budget that justifies taxes on 'bad' goods must also consider the negative effects of taxes on 'good' goods.

Consideration of the negative effects of taxation brings us to the original assumption for this proposal mentioned in the introduction, namely that taxes on Labour and the products of Labour tend to discourage production. Thus the requirement to reform over 80% of government revenue may be said to stem from a mere requirement of logical consistency on the part of the finance minister. Given that he has the material welfare of the citizens at heart, any finance minister is thereby obliged to abolish all taxes on the production of 'good' goods.

Method of abolition

There are two general methods by which this taxation may be phased out. A, Reduce all taxes a little in each budget so that they all finally disappear in the last budget. B, Abolish one tax after another.

Method A suffers from the fact that there would be no administrative relief until the final reduction. B allows administrative relief to be spread over each budget, giving time for personnel relocation, as well as cutting some administrative costs in each budget.

Method B is preferred in general, but because of its over-whelming predominance (collecting nearly a half of all revenue) Income tax has to be treated by Method A. All income related taxes are collected under the 'P.A.Y.E. System' so they can be treated as one tax. Because of its structure, the best method of removing this tax seems to be to progressively raise the zero tax threshold for all the various levies simultaneously. This would free those on lowest incomes first, at the same time as it benefited those on higher wage levels.

Irish Government (Central and Local) Revenue 1987

	£m	% of total revenue
Income tax	2,713	
Employment and training levy	97	
Income levy	3	
P.R.S.I and other levies	1,102	
Total income taxes	3,915	48.4
VAT	1,585	19.6
Road Fuel excise	439*	5.4
Alcohol excise	381*	4.7
Local authority service charges	330*	4.1
Tobacco excise	303*	3.7
Corporation profits	257	3.2
Rates	170	2.1
Excises on cars and parts	140	1.7
Customs	88	1.1
Insurance and bank levies	85	1.1
Stamp duties on Land and property	59	0.7
Excises on non road fuels	58	0.7
Capital acquisitions tax	25	0.3
Betting duties	18*	0.2
Table waters excise	15	0.2
Capital gains tax	13	0.16
Cheques and bills stamp duties	12	0.15
Agricultural levies	11	0.14
Stocks and share s stamp duties	7	0.09
Foreign travel excise	7	0.09
Companies Capital duties	6	0.07
Television excise	5.4	0.07
Dance licences, etc.	3*	0.04
Video excise	2.4	0.03
Residential property tax	2.1	0.03
Firearms licences	2*	0.03
Gramophone record excise	1.1	0.01
Mechanical lighters excise	0.5	0.005
Estate duties	0.5	0.005
Matches	0.5	0.005
Others	17	0.2
	£8,096m	c.100 %

* These are to remain.

Considerations for the order of abolition

The situation in Ireland, consistent with most western nations, is that there are a large number of different taxes (see table) each of which affects production in its own way. While it is probable that every tax has champions for its primary removal, a serious budget proposal must consider a number of different questions: A, the cost to the exchequer of collecting the particular tax in proportion to the revenue it raises: its 'administrative efficiency'. B, the effect of the tax on the alternative revenue raiser, and C, the social destructiveness of each tax. D, cross-border trade problems may also have to be taken into account in some special cases.

A Administrative efficiency

It is not generally realised that the collection efficiency of individual taxes can vary enormously. Generally speaking, the more revenue raised by a particular tax, the more efficient it is. For example, VAT and Income tax cost about 1 and 2% (1982 figures) of their respective revenues, while Capital Acquisitions tax, Capital gains tax and Estate duties combined cost 14% of revenue (1982 figures).

Some taxes are inherently more costly than others, e.g. Income tax is twice as costly (2%) as VAT (1%) though it raises twice as much revenue.

There is, of course, compliance cost involved in all revenue raising. It is probably sufficient to surmise that compliance costs are likely to be proportional to the administrative costs. Therefore to arrive at a figure for 'unproductive' costs associated with revenue raising we may double the administrative costs. Thus Income tax costs 4%, VAT 2% and Capital taxes 28% (1982).

On this consideration alone then it would seem that the smaller taxes should be abolished before the larger, more efficient, ones.

B Affect on alternative revenue

Some taxes discourage the sale or transfer of real estate, thereby distorting and reducing the market in real estate. And since the alternative revenue raiser depends on accurate valuation of ground values, such taxes must be removed as the alternative is implemented; these include Capital gains tax, Capital acquisitions tax and stamp duties on property.

Some taxes bear a superficial resemblance to the alternative revenue source making it politically expedient to remove them at the time that the alternate source is introduced; these include Rates and Residential property tax.

C Social destructiveness

If it is a difficult task to choose between two evils, it is even more difficult to arrange a series of them in ascending order. Yet this must be the purpose of this paper if maximum advantage is to be gained from the project.

Having taken the previous two considerations into account, the choice appears to be between those taxes levied directly on Labour and those on production in general. Though both cause unemployment *and* general impoverishment, the Labour taxes cause unemployment *directly* and general impoverishment *indirectly*; taxes on production function in reverse.

Although individuals would probably cite impoverishment (lack of money) as their greatest bane, on a national level unemployment must surely take the laurels as the greater evil. So it seems that taxes on Labour must go before those on general production.

D Special cases

The argument for the reduction or elimination of certain taxes to remove cross border advantage is a very strong one, as the cost to the exchequer will be small compared to the many benefits of keeping trade within our borders. And even if the exchequer cost would not be directly 'self-financing' (because of greater revenue on greater internal trade in those goods), it is likely to be indirectly self-financing (greater revenue on internal trade taken as a whole).

So strong is this argument that it is likely that much will be done to amend the situation in the near future. Motor vehicles and electrical goods are two examples of the problem.

The order for abolition

Firstly, there are those taxes whose removal will greatly expedite the implementation of the alternative revenue source. These are Capital acquisitions tax, Capital gains tax, Stamp duties on property, Residential property tax and Rates. Only Rates is a significant revenue raiser.

Secondly, there are a number of taxes whose contribution to the exchequer is so small that to remove them completely would do little to the overall revenue total, but would give considerable administrative and compliance relief. Any tax that collects less than a ¼ of 1 per cent would fall into this category.

The first major tax to go would be income tax. It is clear that this could not be removed in a single budget; three or more budgets would be required.

Finally there are those taxes on general or particular trades and production processes. Taking these in ascending order of revenue raised, they are: Excises on non road fuels, Insurance and Bank levies, Customs, Motor vehicle licences, Excises on cars and parts, Corporation profits tax, and Value Added Tax. All (with the possible exception of VAT) are small enough that one or more could be removed per year.

Budget strategy

Assuming a government elected with a mandate to implement this reform, the following two strategies show annual budgets for two different lengths of office. The first is five years, the maximum government term prescribed under the Electoral Act of 1963; the second is seven years, the maximum government term prescribed in the Irish Constitution. The rate of change is envisaged as accelerating each year.

Strategy I

A five year term of office

		£m
Budget 1	Capital Gains tax	13
	Capital Acquisitions tax	25
	Stamp duties on property	59
	Residential property tax	2
	Rates	170
	All taxes less than ¼% of revenue	70
	Income tax reduction	661
		1,000
Budget 2	Income tax reduction	1,200
Budget 3	Income tax reduction	1,400
Budget 4	Income tax abolished	654
	Non Road fuel excises	58
	Insurance and Bank levies	85
	Customs	88
	Vehicle licences	139
	Excises on cars and parts	140
		1,421
Budget 5	Abolish VAT	1,585

Strategy II
A seven year term of office

		£m
Budget 1	Capital Gains tax	13
	Capital Acquisition tax	25
	Stamp duties on property	59
	Residential property tax	2
	Rates	170
	All taxes less than ¼% of revenue	70
	Income tax reduction	361
		700
Budget 2	Income tax reduction	750
Budget 3	Income tax reduction	800
Budget 4	Income tax reduction	850
Budget 5	Income tax reduction	900
Budget 6	Abolish income tax	254
	Excises on non road fuels	58
	Insurance and Bank levies	85
	Customs	88
	Vehicle licences	139
	Excise on cars and parts	140
	Corporations profits tax	257
		1,021
Budget 7	Abolish VAT	1,585

Strategy III

The above two strategies show the order of abolition of taxes, ideal from a government point of view. It will be noticed that the budget changes are rather large – £700m is the smallest. This might incur sheer logistical problems, not to mention social disruption. Smaller budget changes would not, however, change the order of abolition except in the first two budgets; these are laid out below. Taking a modest rate of change per year of £350m – as here shown – it would take nineteen years to complete the reform.

		£m
Budget 1	Residential property tax	2
	Capital Gains tax	13
	Capital Acquisitions tax	25
	Stamp duties on property	59
	Rates reduction	70
	Income tax reduction	181
		350
Budget 2	Rates abolition	100
	All taxes less than ¼% of revenue	70
	Income tax reduction	180
		350

Budgets 3-19   Reduce income taxes to zero, then remove VAT

Potential for reduced government requirement

The potential for a reduction in government requirements comes from two main sources.

Firstly, the replacement of over thirty separate taxes by a single one would, of itself, reduce administrative costs. Furthermore, the simplicity and unavoidability of the new source would make it very inexpensive to administer. The annual saving is likely to be in the order of £80m.

Secondly and more significantly would be the reduced need for government activity in many areas of the economy due to the incentive effects of removing taxation. A conservative estimate of this saving would be about £1,000m. This could be a considerable underestimate as this is the nub of the reform: it is the whole point of making this dramatic change in the first place. A saving of £3,000m might not be out of the question.

Thus it is improbable that the new revenue source would have to yield £6.6 billion. Half of that figure might be closer to the required target.

Putting figures on it

Presentation of budgets are frequently accompanied by examples of how the changes proposed will affect particular individuals/families/ industries, etc. Such examples will not be given because they normally only show the first effects of the change, and do not show the myriad of knock on effects, particularly effects on incentives. This, as the great French statesman and journalist Frederic Bastiat demonstrated more than a century ago in his timeless essay, 'What is seen, and what is not seen', is the single greatest barrier to clear economic understanding. Indeed, it is the most misleading method of economic analysis possible. Unless one analyses every single knock on effect of the proposal, the practice of giving selected examples should be considered suspect.

All that can be said is that the reform will have certain general effects (in this case in wealth creation and reduced government requirements); exactly how the 'higgling' of the market place will sort things out is simply not knowable.

Two further comments may be added. (i) The proposed revenue source, properly implemented, will allow the free market to allocate the charge distribution (see Raising Revenue without Taxation). It is obviously impossible to say exactly how the free market will act. (ii) This reform is likely to change fundamentally the whole pattern of economic development, so that any interpolation from the present pattern is likely to be wide of the mark.

Acknowledgements

I wish to thank the following for permission to reproduce portraits in this book: The Central Zionist Archive in Jerusalem for Franz Oppenheimer (page 25); Bettmann/CORBIS, copyright owners of the portrait of John Locke (page 45); Harvard University for Robert Nozick (page 143); and Buckingham University for Norman Barry (page 143). The remaining portraits are in the public domain.

Bibliography

Anderson, Philip, *The Secret Life of Real Estate*: *How it moves and why* , London, Shepheard-Walwyn, 2008.

Bandow, Doug, *Beyond Good Intentions*: *A Biblical view of politics*, Crossway Books, 1988.

Barry, Norman P., *On Classical Liberalism and Libertarianism*, St. Martin's Press, New York, 1987.

Bastiat, Frederick, *The Law,* The Foundation for Economic Education, New York, 1984 (1850).

Caroll, Lewis, *Through the Looking Glass,* Oxford University Press, World's Classics, 1998 (1872).

Dowd, Kevin, *Laissez Faire Banking,* Routledge, London, 1993.

Gaffney, Mason and Harrison, Fred, *The Corruption of Economics,* Shepheard-Walwyn, London, 1994.

Garrison, William Lloyd, www.theliberatorfiles.com/oughtness-of-life-primary-for-garrison/.

George, Henry, *Progress and Poverty*, Robert Schalkenbach Foundation, New York, 2003 (1879).

George, Henry, *A Perplexed Philosopher,* Robert Schalkenbach Foundation, New York, 1937 (1892).

Gwartney, Ted, *Incentive Taxation,* Centre for the Study of Economics, 1988, www.urbantoolsconsult.org.

Hayek, F.A., *The Constitution of Liberty,* Routledge & Keegan Paul, London, 1976 (1960).

Heilbroner, Robert, *The New Yorker*, January 1989.

Herodytus, *The History,* Book iii, par. 80, *c.*450 BC. Also see Wikipedia, 'Isonomia'.

Hobbes, Thomas, *Leviathan,* Yale University Press, 2010 (1651).

Horsman, Michael, *Raising Revenue Without Taxation*, private publication, 1984.

Locke, John, *The Second Treatise on Civil Government*, Prometheus Books, New York, 1986 (1690).

Mandeville, Bernard, *The Fable of The Bees,* Wishart & Company, London, 1934 (1714).

Marx, Karl, *Das Capital,* Encyclopaedia Britannica, Great Books of the Western World, 1988 (1867).

McEachran, Frank, *Freedom – The Only End,* Johnson Publications, London, 1966.

Montesquieu, Charles Louis, *The Spirit of The Laws,* Hafner/Macmillan Publishers, 1949 (1748).

Nock, Albert Jay, *Our Enemy, The State,* Hallberg Publications, Wisconsin, 1983 (1935).

Nozick, Robert, *Anarchy, State, and Utopia,* Basic Books, New York, 1974.

Oppenheimer, Franz, *The State,* Free Life Editions, New York, 1975 (1908, tr. 1914).

Regan, Ronald, 'A Time for Choosing' (speech), October 27, 1964.

Rousseau, Jean Jacques, *The Social Contract,* Dover Thrift Editions, New York, 2003 (1762).

Rushdoony, Rousas John, *Politics of Guilt and Pity,* Ross House Books, California, 1995 (1970).

Rustow, Alexander, *Freedom and Domination,* Princeton University Press, 1950 (tr. 1980).

Selgin, George, *The Theory of Free Banking,* Rownan & Littlefield, New Jersey, 1988.

Selgin, George, *Bank Deregulation and Monetary Order,* Routledge, London & New York, 1996.

Sennholz, Hanz F., *Money and Freedom,* Libertarian Press, Pennsylvania, 1985.

Shakespeare, William, *The Rape of Lucrece,* The Illustrated Stratford Shakespeare, Chancellor Press, London, 1987 (1687).

Smith, Adam, *The Wealth of Nations,* Encyclopaedia Britannica, Great Books of the Western World, 1988 (1776).

Spencer, Herbert, *Social Statics,* Augustus M. Kelley, New York, 1969 (1851).

Spencer, Herbert, *The Proper Sphere of Government,* Letter X, Liberty Classics, Indianapolis, 1981 (1843).

Defoe, Daniel, *Robinson Crusoe,* Penguin Books, London, 2003 (1719).

Tolstoy, Count Leo, *A Great Iniquity,* Free Age Press, London, 1905.

Ueda, Kazuo, *The Japanese Banking Crisis in the 1990s,* 1998, www.bis.org/publ/plcy07q.pdf.

Von Mises, Ludwig, *The Theory of Money and Credit,* Liberty Classics, Indianapolis, 1981 (1912, tr. 1934).

Webber, Maz, *Politics as a Vocation,* Hacket Publishing Co., Indianapolis/Cambridge, 2004 (1919).

Biblical References

(New International Version)

Leviticus 19: 18	Love your Neighbour.
Leviticus 25: 14-16 & 23	Land property rights.
Deuteronomy 5: 6-21	Thou shalt not steal. Ten Commandments.
1 Samuel 8: 6	First King ends Judges period.
1 Samuel 12: 17	First King ends Judges period.
Nehemiah, Chapter 5	The governor rails against upper class oppression.
Psalm 115: 16	The earth is given by God to Man.
Isaiah 5: 8	Woe to Land Speculators.
Isaiah 42: 4	He will establish Justice on Earth.
Daniel, Chapter 6.	Daniel refuses to worship the State and survives the Lions.
Amos 5: 24	Let Justice roll on like a river.
Malachi 4: 2	As free and happy as calves released from the stall.
Matthew 17: 24-27	The Temple tax in the fish's mouth.
Matthew 22: 15-22	Render unto Caesar.
Matthew Chapter 23	Woe to the hypocritical religious leaders.
Mark 12: 31	Love your neighbour.
John 10: 10	Jesus to give life to the full.
Revelation 13: 4	Who is like the beast?
Revelation 13: 8	Those not written in the book of life will worship the beast

Resources

The Single Tax
aka. Land Value Tax, LVT, Site Value Tax, etc.

Robert Schalkenbach Foundation, 211 East 43rd Street, Suite 400, New York, NY 10017. Telephone: 212-683-6424; toll-free 800-269-9555. Fax: 212-683-6454. Email: info@schalkenbach.org www.schalkenbach.org

The International Union for Land Value Taxation and Free Trade, www.theiu.org

Mason Gaffney, Professor Emeritus of Economics, University of California, Riverside, www.masongaffney.org

The Minimal State

The Foundation for Economic Education, 30 South Broadway, Irvington, NY 10533. Main Line: 914-591-7230. www.fee.org

www.bastiat.org/en/

The Free Judicial Service

Nothing that I am aware of; please contact me if you know of anything.

Free Banking or Laissez-Fair Banking

www.freebanking.org

WWW.THESTATEOFFREEDOMANDJUSTICE.COM

michael@sofaj.org

Mobile: 00353 86 088 2515. Landline: 00353 402 24505

Index